WITH FERVOR BURNING

BY

HILARION M. HENARES, JR.

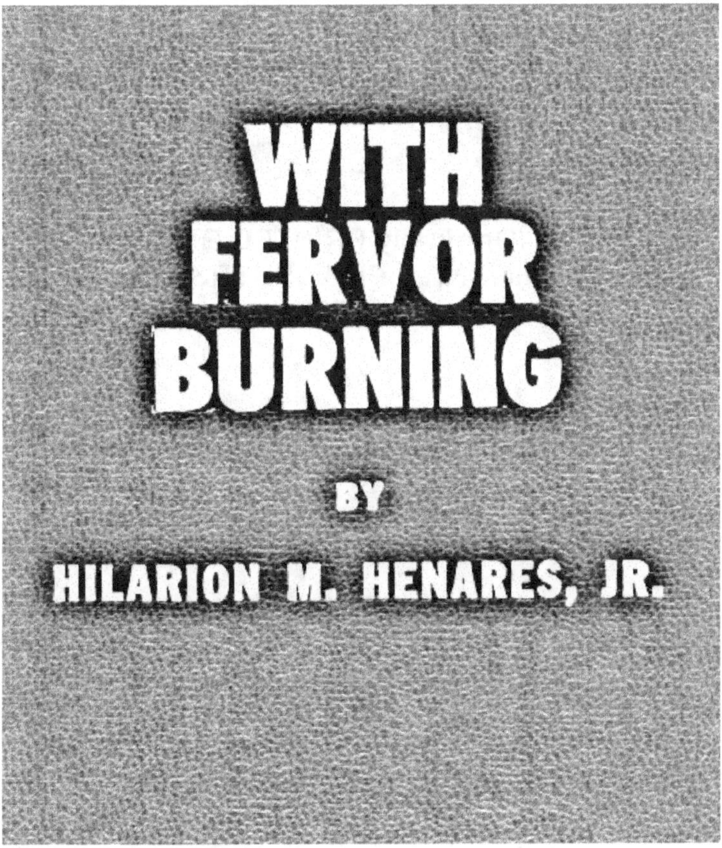

Original Edition, 1965
Re-issue, 2017

DEDICATION:

To my sons:

HILARION (Ronnie),

ALFREDO TOMAS (Atom)
and

DANIEL GUILLERMO (Danby)

With these words to live by:
"The world will step aside for any man
who knows where he is going."

ACKNOWLEDGEMENT

To the Manila Times in which these
articles have originally appeared in
its Ways and Means column. And
to Rex De Garcia Lores who arduously
pored over the proofs and saw this
book through the press.

---

*Lei not Macaulay's traveller from New Zealand
exploring the spectral ruins of Manila in the course
of his post-atomic war peregrinations, and
cautiously testing the radioactive waters of the
Pasig, from the broken arches of the Quezon
bridge, have cause to ponder that in those
shattered tenements and poisoned fields and rivers
once lived a nation unique in the annals of mankind,
free men who put their liberties on the auction
block, a sacrificial race with a mysterious urge to
suicide who, being weak and weaponless took upon
themselves the quarrels of the
strong, and having been warned of their
abandonment still persisted in their lonely course,
and whose brutalised and monstrously deformed
survivors, scrambling with stunted limbs in the
infected debris of their liberated cities, had
forgotten even the echo of the memory of the
strsinge illusion for which their race had
fought and perished.*

CLARO M. RECTO

Hilarion (Larry) M. Henares Jr.   **3**

What they say

I read practically all the leading articles on economic studies and I recall distinctly that among the articles that I read there stood out as exemplary in their sense, in their learning, and in their intelligence the articles of one who is truly one of the authorities in economics in our country — Hilarion M. Henares, Jr.

PRESIDENT DIOSDADO MACAPAGAL

The highest-paid cabinet member, Henares wields tremendous economic power and influence, second perhaps only to the President

PHILIPPINES FREE PRESS

One of the most fascinating personalities in politics today is Hilarion M. Henares, Jr. He is an engaged intellectual whose vision and profundity are beyond question.

Like the character Herzog in Saul Bellow's novel, his validity and depth spring from his monologue and conversation with the inner self.

ANDRES CRISTOBAL CRUZ
(Author, TOYM Awardee in Literature)

Henares' writings clearly indicate the tone and magnitude basic philosophy and ideas. Whether it be in economics, or his more intense moments, in matters affecting the dilemma man himself in this mechanized world, Henares displays a passion for truth and an intelligence capable of assimilating seemingly disparate aspects of culture and presenting them in the coherence of a solid logical structure.

CARLOS P. ROMULO

In our country, Larry Henares, Jr. represents the Wave of the Future.

FRED MANGAHAS **(Columnist)**

ABOUT THE AUTHOR

One of the most phenomenal careers in private enterprise in this country is probably that of Hilarion M. Henares, Jr., presently the Chairman of the economic planning arm of the government, the National Economic Council.

At the age of twenty-five, he was dean of a graduate school in a university. Before he was thirty, he made his first million as a head of a vast business consortium making no less than 56 products. He is the youngest Chairman of the National Economic Council, and the highest paid cabinet member.

He attended the rigid Jesuit school of Ateneo de Manila where he finished his secondary education. He continued to formalize his education at the University of the Philippines. Later, he attended the Massachusetts Institute of Technology where he graduated with a degree in Business and Engineering Administration.

He was former president of the Philippine Chamber of Industries, founder and President of the Association of Management and Industrial Engineers of the Philippines, founder and Vice-President of the Philippine Council of Management, founder and head of Feati Graduate School of Management Engineering, founder and Vice-Dean of the School of Commerce of the Lyceum of the Philippines, President of H. G. Henares and Sons, Inc., President of the Amalgamated Specialties Corporations and others. He has also participated in various world conferences involving trade, finance and economic affairs.

CONTENTS

PREFACE

Some people concentrate on one special field and become successful after a lifetime of hard work. Hilarion M. Henares, Jr, can be said to have been leaping from crag to crag and from peak to peak in many different fields, and has achieved success in each of them incredible for a man of his tender years.

He obtained his training at the Massachusetts Institute of Technology where he distinguished himself with a high scholastic record. At the age of 25 he was the youngest Dean of a private graduate school. Before thirty he was the head of an industrial complex making 56 different products and was subsequently elected president of the Philippine Chamber of Industries. He made one movie and it won the coveted award of "'the best documentary film of the year." He and his family also received the distinction of having been chosen as the year's exemplary family.

Henares rightly deserves what Dr. Lilian Gilbreth said of him: "the father of Management Revolution in the Philippines."

Henares is a writer, and may be considered one of our liberal intellectuals. His passion for nationalism and the widening of the forces and benefits of democracy to improve the lot of our masses he has made the controlling principle in his official acts.

Henares' confident faith in our people's capacity to rise and fulfill the expectations of Dr. Jose Rizal, if embodied in a political action can, with the support and gathering of a mass movement, inexorably usher him in the center of the historical process.

It is often said that the twentieth century is the century of revolutions. But most importantly, the 1960's saw a new kind of leadership asserted, such as that of President Kennedy in the American scene and Prime Minister Wilson in England.

The Old Order is passing from the scene and we

are witnessing a general intellectual and social ferment the implications of which are likely to re-shape our institutions, our concept of values, the structures of our economic and social life.

This slim volume clearly indicates the tone and magnitude of Henares' basic philosophy and ideas. Whether it be in economics, or in his more intense moments, in matters affecting the dilemma of man himself in this mechanized world, Henares displays a passion for truth and an intelligence capable of assimilating seemingly disparate aspects of culture and presenting them in the coherence of a solid logical structure.

In the manner of the celebrated dramatist, Eugene Ionesco, Henares does not stop asking questions, a supreme quality which is characteristic of an engaging and living mind. And in the questions he asks, we are able to perceive the glimmer of the significance of the human effort in our own society and time. This, I believe, is what makes for the cogency and importance of the present volume.

January 26, 1965

CARLOS P. ROMULO

THE MAGNIFICENT FAILURE

He was born poor and despised. But he was good and gentle and just.

He was full of ideas, great ideas that threatened to topple an empire, ideas that were to change the face of the earth.

He was a real revolutionary. He was like the communists in a certain sense, in that he wanted everyone to get a share of the wealth of the world.

But unlike the communists, he did not say "What is yours, is mine." He said, "What is mine, is yours!"

Because he was an agitator, he incurred the disfavor of men of wealth and political power. They drove him out of their cities. They beat him up and called him a fool, and set the police on his friends.

Finally they arrested him. A friend betrayed him. The rest of his friends deserted him. And he went through the mockery of a trial.

His enemies tortured him, and when they got tired of doing that, they sent him to die like a common criminal. While he was dying, his executioners gambled for the only piece of property he had on earth, and that was his tattered robe.

Was he a failure, this man they called Jesus Christ?

But the story does not end there. For soon after he died, this man did topple empires, did change the face of the earth. And even now, his influence is felt in every nation, in every city, in the heart of every man.

Those of us who feel the bitterness and frustration of a lost cause should take heart from the final triumph of such a magnificent "failure."

NEW FACE, NEW YEAR, NEW RESOLVE

Without eyeglasses, a myopic man looks better — and all the girls he looks at also look better. So, being happily married and with every intention to continue being so, X put my glasses back on and lo, there is a new face in this space.

The eyeglasses bring into focus the crisp new calendar on the wall, still fresh with the smell of printer's ink, with all its days neatly laid out in squares, numbered in sequence and parcelled out among the coming months of the New Year.

The clink of wine glasses, the toasts, the kisses, the toots of horns, the blast of miniature bombs, the laughter and gaiety of the night before —now give way
to the bleary weary reappraisal of the morning after — then, inevitably, to the renewed hopes and determined resolutions of the coming tomorrow.

The New Year is not just one day, but a whole year of 364 virgin dawns awaiting the seductive stroke of number less New Year's resolutions. Here goes:

First of all, we here highly resolve to renew our allegiance to the Republic of the Philippines, and to no other country, no matter how friendly, wealthy or powerful. We shall promote and defend the interests of our country and our citizens, just as assiduously as foreign embassies protect the interests of their respective countries and citizens.

Secondly, we reiterate our faith in the Filipino, in his competence to take care of his own affairs, and in his capacity for greatness. We resolve never to let pass unchallenged any alien-induced notion that our ultimate destiny lies in the hands of those other than ourselves. For we believe strongly that only when we have confidence in ourselves do we inspire the confidence of others. In the great drama of nation-building, we

With Fervor Burning

Filipinos must assume the starring role; everyone else must be in the supporting cast.

Thirdly, we shall preach hope. We resolve never to join the professional prophets of doom in the current fad of national self-flagellation. For we who would transform a nation and renovate a stagnant society, cannot do 90 by driving the people to despair, nor by stirring up and captaining discontent, nor by infecting the people with self-doubt, fear or hatred, nor by submitting ourselves in humility and humiliation to the guidance and judgment of foreign mentors. We must learn somehow to kindle and fan an extravagant hope with which to inspire our own people to constructive action.

Fourth, we shall, "agitate the very core of the national spirit," usher our people into a sense of self-involvement, a sense of conscious participation in the actions and passions of our times. We shall direct our message not only to the intellectual, but to the industrialist, the merchant, the jeepney driver, the laborer, the student, the farmer and every common tao — echoing the words of one philosopher:

"There are no great men. There are only great challenges which fate forces ordinary men to face."

Fifth, we resolve to comport ourselves according to the principles of democratic liberalism that every idea may meet the challenge of other ideas in free, open and unlimited debate. We are against subversive acts, not heretical thoughts; for what is heresy to some may be truth to others. And we certainly deplore the subversive activities of alien-inspired Communists, McCarthyists, Goldwaterites end Manchurian Candidates who squat on our soil and befoul the air with fear, hatred, distrust and intolerance.

For we may disagree without being disagreeable. And personally, I resolve to adhere religiously to the tenets of the Society to which I have just been inducted — the SPCA, that is, the Society for the Prevention of Cruelty to Americans.

Finally, I resolve in deference to readers and with due apologies to professional colleagues — in promulgating my esoteric cogitations or articulating my sentimentalities, to shun all platitudinous ponderosity; to eschew all conglomerations of flatulent garrulity, jejune babblement and asinine affectations; to renounce all polysyllabic profundity, setaceous vacuity and grandiloquent vapidity — in other words, I shall write simply, clearly, sincerely and above all, avoid using big words.

For big words do not necessarily reflect grand thoughts. And it is a presumptuous ambition of ours to have it said of this column, as was once said of Churchill:

"By saying simply and plainly what we feel, he enabled us to feel it still more strongly, has driven us to the limits of our potentialities and has given us a vision of our own best possibilities."

THE WONDER OF MY FATHER

October 21, is the birthday of my father. With the indulgence of the reader, of him I shall write.

He is a man of many passions, and he had the restless, relentless, persistent and energetic determination to pursue them at all cost and over all obstacles.

One of his greatest passions was the love he bore for Miss Concepcion Q. Maramba who, after a courtship that lasted three years and spanned two continents, finally consented to be his wife.

He turned out to be a henpecked husband, and proud of it: "We Henareses are born to command legions' of men and we can afford to let our wives dominate us. Only the man who gets kicked around in the office comes home at night to beat up his wife out of sheer frustration."

Because he is henpecked, it is not surprising that it was not he who started the family business. It was his wife. But he eventually took over the management of the enterprise and turned it into a multi-million peso industrial complex.

"Papa, why do we have a factory? People make so much more money just buying and selling!"

"Well, son," my father replied, It is a lot easier to buy-and-sell than it is to buy-make-and-sell. But I'll tell you why I got into manufacturing. It is because of the satisfaction I derive from it. You see, son, if I buy something and then sell it, the price increases but the value does not change, for I sell only what I buy.

"But if I buy, let us say a pound of steel costing 20 centavos and make 20,000 pesos worth of watch springs out of it, something new has been added.

"The value has increased. Why? Because of the work I put into it; because I add into that pound of steel a part of myself — the skill of my hands, the knowledge of my mind and the pride in my heart. I create something that was not there before. And son, somehow, I feel like a little god!"

Indeed, the one other great passion of his life is the Industrial Revolution in his own country. An engineer with three degrees, he attracted nation-wide attention as "the Most Prolific Filipino Inventor," did most of the pioneering work for the diversification of the sugar and coconut industries. He invented such machines and labor-saving devices as sack-making equipment, rat-duster, locust sprayer, fertilizer applicator; made industrial alcohol, liquors, bottles, fertilizer from sugar byproducts; also soap, coir bags, insecticide, insulating board, candies, coco milk from what he lovingly called "the tree of life," the coconut tree.

He developed the famous IPOIPI charcomobile

With Fervor Burning

which runs cars and trucks on coconut charcoal, and solved the transportation problem (especially the transportation of food) during the Japanese occupation.

He organized the Philippine Chamber of Industries, one of the most powerful and militant organizations today. He went further. Because he wanted to bring industrialization to the very grassroots of the country's economy, he pioneered in the Home Industries Movement ("If you can swim in six feet of water, you can swim in water six miles deep!").

Looking across the years, I cannot help seeing how much my father influenced the course of my life.

Once, while I was brooding on some shameful deed, he put his arms around me and ever so gently said: "Please remember that nothing you can ever do, however evil, can ever make me love you less. If you ever get into trouble, never hesitate to tell me about it And we shall see together how we can set the matter right and prevent it from ever happening again."

I remember his advice after I graduated from college: "Earn as much money as you can, son. When the time comes that money is of no more importance to you, when the time comes that money becomes only a means of keeping score in the great game of business, then retire. Retire during the most productive period of your life, and offer your time and talent to the service of your country. For the greatest gratification any man can have is to make his mark upon history."

A writer named Carlos Bulosan once wrote of the laughter of his father. I now write of the wonder of my father. Not only because, to me and to many others, he is a wonderful man, but also because he is a man so full of wonder — full of the wonder of life itself, its challenges, its excitement, its grandeur and the innate goodness of its ultimate purpose. Full of the wonder of love which he lavished, without counting the cost, on his family, his friends, his fellow industrialists, and above all, way above all, his native land.   -----

MAIN GOAL, MOTIVE POWER

For centuries past until not so long ago, the Filipino *tao* dwelt in the pastoral peace of a plantation economy. He was the quiescent and inarticulate victim of poverty, ignorance, and injustice. Heaven on earth, he thought, was reserved for landlords, priests and men of lighter skin.

But no longer. Today the Filipino *tao* no longer believes that poverty, ignorance and injustice are predestined conditions of earthly existence. He knows now, as surely as he brushes his teeth with dental cream and hears about reports from Manila, that a better life is possible for himself and his children.

The Filipino *tao* is not alone. All over the world, especially among the nations of South America, Africa and Asia, there is in progress a "revolution of rising expectations," a revolution more global in its scope, more basic and more far-reaching in its effects than either the French, the American or the Russian revolutions.

Such a revolution has for its major manifestations two mighty movements: the quest for Industrialization and the rise of Nationalism.

It is Industrialization that breaks down and transforms primitive feudal societies into a highly organized social order characterized by the employment of large scale labor and machinery, mass production and mass consumption. It is Industrialization that promises a higher standard of living for a growing population.

But Industrialization necessarily involves sacrifice — sacrifice in the limitation of consumption goods to satisfy the insatiable demand for capital investment, sacrifice to endure the painful readjustments in traditional attitudes, habits and way of life.

It is Nationalism that inspires the selfless

dedication to accept such temporary sacrifices for the long-term benefits of industrialization. It is Nationalism that gives us the self-confidence to strive for the best, the creative conceit that makes possible the impossible; the self-identity and togetherness to unite us in common purpose toward a common destiny.

Industrialization then provides the means and Nationalism provides the motive power for our nation's progress and prosperity — even as in the rest of the world, where steel mills, dams and modem factories have replaced temples and monuments as the outward symbols of national grandeur.

THE FILIPINO ENTREPRENEUR

If industrialization provides the engine of progress and nationalism, the motive power, who then is the prime mover, the man at the wheel?

In almost all the emerging nations of Asia and Africa, the state is the prime mover of economic progress. For sickened by centuries of colonial exploitation, the new nations are determined to rely primarily on their own resources for the task of nation-building. But in a poor underdeveloped country, only the state can raise the capital, assume the risk, and supply the organization for economic development Thus in many emerging nations the state reigns supreme at the expense of the individual.

But in the Philippines, by a unique turn of events, the individual emerges with a promise of great expectations in a new type of man — a truly indigenous breed — the Filipino entrepreneur.

Who is he? Who is this Filipino entrepreneur?

His name or position does not matter much. For he comes from all walks of life, cutting across traditional class barriers with the ease of social mobility. He is at once a lowly *cochero* who parlayed a remnant store into a textile mill complex; a member of a brotherhood of undertakers undertaking to build an oil refinery; a landed aristocrat setting up a poor man's university and a flour mill.

Who is he?

In a society bound by tradition, he is the innovator, seeking out new business relationships, new products to make, new techniques of production, new methods of marketing, new markets.

In a frivolous society, he is the thinker and doer, the organizer who puts men, money, and machines together in productive and profitable relationship.

In a society of desperate job-seekers, he is the self-confident job-creator who makes decisions, takes risks and accepts responsibility.

In a society hypnotized by dogmas and slogans and blinded by feudal loyalties, he has a mind of his own and the courage to speak it out, through a myriad organizations, insistent, demanding to be heard — for he is intellectually independent. He is intellectually independent because, to a large degree, he is financially independent, unlike the parasitic *ilustrado* or the apathetic *tao*, he has developed a certain amount of self-reliance, initiative, resourcefulness and a talent for organization.

In a society anesthesized by a colonial mentality and double allegiance, he is a nationalist of the highest order who loves his country above all else and can stand up to all the world and say "I am a Filipino and an Asian."

The Filipino entrepreneur and his Schumpeterian cluster of followers, along with the burgeoning middle class of professionals and factory workers that follows in their wake, are indeed the agents and prime movers of economic progress.

They are the pregnant minority who bear the foetus of a new democratic industrial society. Striding the gap between the idle rich and the jobless poor, they are the industrial middle class that guarantee stability to our democratic way of life.

THE FILIPINA AS ENTREPRENEUR

The women of the Philippines occupy n position in the social structure, which is probably the most unique in the world.

A female child born to a Filipino family is welcomed as a sign of good fortune, and the sanctity of her person is guarded with almost fanatical zeal by grandmothers and old aunts. And no wonder. When the time comes for her to get married, the man of her choice must prove himself worthy by offering one year's labor free of charge to the girl's parents; he must pay large sums of money to all sorts of relatives as a token of gratitude for their having raised the girl especially for him to love. And all this before the girl is even committed to marry him. When the formal engagement is announced, the man is expected to build a house for the bride, and to give her a complete wardrobe, starting from the comb she wears in her hair progressively down to shoes for her feet. Then when the wedding comes, the man or his family pays for all the expenses of the ceremony from the bridal gown to the wedding feast.

It is the Filipino man who provides the marriage dowry, not the woman. And this practice is known nowhere else in the world, not in the authoritarian societies of the rest of Asia, not even in the liberal-minded nations of the West where women first won the battle for political equality.

The difference does not end there. In the United States and elsewhere, the man comes home with the paycheck, gives the household allowance to his wife and school allowances to his children, and keeps the rest in the bank in his own name. It is the man who does the family saving and investment.

It is not so in the Philippines. The Filipino comes home with the paycheck and gives it to the wife; and it is the wife who gives the children and the husband their allowances. The man is the breadwinner, and he often has to hire himself out to an office or factory to get a steady income. The woman is the keeper of the keys to the exchequer, and it is in this role that she often finds herself an investor and a risk taker.

The more enterprising woman takes the family savings and goes into business — a small store under the house, a cottage industry or even a pawn shop. She may not always succeed, but if she does, the chances are that she makes more money than her husband, and finds so little time left for the family that she asks her husband to leave his job and manage the business for her. And that's how most family fortunes are started — by women. But the Filipino woman will never admit this, not in a manner that might rob her husband of his prerogatives of being lord of the manor.

A woman, after she is married, is especially suited to be an entrepreneur and manager. How many times have you heard such a question directed to a woman: "How do you ever manage on your husband's salary?" And how many times did you hear the answer: "Oh, well, by the grace of God, I manage somehow!"

Well, that is what a wife really does, she manages. And she manages somehow because she has the kind of generalized knowledge that a professional manager ought to have to manage professionally.

A man is forced by outside competition to be a specialist in his field, either as a lawyer, accountant, or some such thing; he is in that sense, one thing to everybody. His wife is everything to somebody; she is a sweetheart of her husband and mother to her children

— but that is not all, she is also the accountant and treasurer of household finances, the judge and jury of family quarrels, the social secretary, the nurse, the psychologist, the cook and the general handy woman for various chores. As such, even as she delegates her work to the servants and the children, she is the general manager of her home.

It is in this light that we may explain the unique role of the Filipino woman as the traditional keeper of savings and investment, the entrepreneur and founder of family fortunes, and as the focal center of home and Philippine society.

TRUTH ABOUT RP INVESTORS

"Filipino investors are shy and timid. Therefore we must depend on foreign investors for pioneering work."

This statement has been repeated so often over and over again like a broken record, that it begins to sound like Goebbel's Truth.

But the gospel truth is that Filipino investors are aggressive, perhaps too aggressive for their own good, considering the alien-induced prejudices to which they are subjected by their own countrymen.

Let's look at the record. Almost every major industry in this country was pioneered by a Filipino.

In the field of food industries, Rose Packing Corporation (organized by Manuel Roxas, father of Sixto, no kin to Gerry) pioneered in general food canning; Darigold (Syjuco) in milk canning; Marcel Packing Corporation in fish canning; Commonwealth Foods in coffee processing; Republic Flour Mills (Araneta) in flour milling. Except for Darigold, all these Filipino pioneers created a market for their own brands in the face of all the odds pitted against what is derogatorily referred to as "locally-made products." The lone pioneer company in this field is the Philippine Packing Corporation (Del Monte) which already had a market in the United States and secured concessions from the government before even risking the start of the venture.

In the textile industry, the Filipino pioneers were the Philippine Cotton Mills in 1930, the National Development Corporation in 1941 and a host of Filipino textile millers who came into the field in the 1950's. The only foreign firm in this field is a late comer, a British firm which is reportedly ready to sell out majority control to Filipinos.

In footwear, Ang Tibay (Toribio Teodoro) and El Porvenir (Geronimo) pioneered in a field that is still dominated by Filipinos. A prewar American firm, Hale Shoe Co., had since gone out of business.

In the field of construction materials: cement manufacture was pioneered by Rizal Cement Corporation; postwar plywood industries by Sta. Clara Lumber Co. (Arevalo and Roces); GI roofing by Puyat Steel; nails and wire products by Marcelo Steel; cast-iron pipes by Antonio Quirino.

Shipbuilding and drydocking were pioneered by NASSCO and El Varadero; steel-making by NASSCO; tinplating by Elizalde; appliances and steel cabinets by Ysmael Steel; soap manufacture by prewar NACOCO; caustic soda and chlorine gas by SUGECO; sulfuric acid by Chemical Industries (Garcia); carbide and polyvinyl chloride by Guevara. Filipinos also pioneered in the manufacture of machine tools, locks, automobile assembly, electric motors (FEATI), and manufacture of parts for cars, tractors and others.

A Filipino pioneer, by the very act of pioneering, is the only one in the field. For this, he is branded as a monopolist, an upstart who "enriches himself by stealing from others" specially when he asks for tariff protection. During the long process of getting the tariff adjusted, he is stymied at every turn by Parkinson lawyers of every stripe.

In the meanwhile, his products are held in contempt as "inferior to foreign brands" and competitive foreign products are imported in massive doses and dumped into the market to drive him out of business.

By the time tariff protection is finally extended, he is exhausted physically, mentally and financially. And he watches helplessly while his foreign competitors, who opposed him to start with, finally puts up a factory of his own amidst public acclamation that "at last a foreign investor has taken an interest in our industrial development."

This has happened more or less in similar manner to Filipino pioneers in the industries of resin, sewing machine, rubber tire, food canning, drug, electric lamp and fertilizer manufacture and other fields.

The paint industry, of which the writer has personal knowledge, deserves special mention here. During the Import Control era, Elizalde & Co. and another Filipino pioneer challenged the Central Bank's "historical pattern of import policy" and demanded that dollar allocations of foreign paint importers be transferred to paint manufacturers on the basis of "total contribution to the economy." After several months of hearings, the Filipino manufacturers indeed won their point.

But the colonial mentality works in strange ways. The Central Bank allowed foreign importers to retain their dollar allocations for use in importing other items. And to add injury to insult, the Central Bank granted the foreign importers additional dollars for machinery and raw materials to manufacture paint Needless to say, the Filipino pioneers lost out to the Johnny-come-lately, importer-turned-manufacturer foreign firms.

The Macapagal Administration has recognized the shortcomings of previous administrations in this respect, and has pledged itself to support the cause of

Filipino investors. Mr. Macapagal is the first President to utilize seriously the Presidential powers (under Section 401 of the Tariff Code) to modify tariff rates. He has issued no less than four tariff proclamations so far (Executive Orders No. 5, 13a. 31 and 66); no other President in all our history has done as much.

No, no, Filipino investors are not timid, they're just intimidated. And the miracle of it all is that they still have the courage to try. And most of them do succeed.

LET'S COUNT OUR BLESSINGS

At every crossroads of history, there are always those who stop, hesitate and turn their backs on the destiny that beckons to them.

During the American Revolution, they were the Tories who professed loyalty to the British at the very time their own country was breaking the shackles of British colonialism.

In Latin America, they are called Malinche, in painful memory of an Indian princess who became the mistress of a Spanish conquistador and masterminded the genocide of her own people.

In colonial India, they were personified by Gunga Din and Sabu, the Elephant Boy.

In contemporary Philippines, they go by many names but there is one characteristic they share — they have lost faith in the Filipino, they have lost confidence in their own people's capacity for greatness.

At the crossroads of our own history, as we set the stage for our Industrial Revolution and economic independence, we hear little but jeers from our own cheering squad — Filipino capital is timid, Filipino businessmen are thieves, Filipino management and labor absolutely inefficient, Filipino products inferior, Filipino politicians are crooks, Filipino nationalists are communists, and the Philippines would be better off as a banana republic for the benefit of colonial trading posts, with its national policies serving a cause "higher" than plain national interest.

The lack of Filipino national pride is probably due to the fact that being the most open society in this part of the world, our country has unwittingly become a "free zone" of competing foreign interests, each claiming superiority over the others in their attempts to influence our ambivalent minds and pocketbooks.

"When bull elephants fight, the grass is trampled upon," so goes an African proverb. And when well-financed, well-organized foreign agencies blow their trumpets, the voices of nationalism are drowned in the uproar, national pride is trampled upon. We have become a nation of Anglophiles, little brown Americans, pro-Japanese, Indonesian lovers, but cursed are of us who express love of country beyond mere lip-service — or we offend our foreign friends and give aid and comfort to our enemies.

Perhaps, now and then, we Filipinos should pause and count our blessings — if only to prove to ourselves that our country is still worth saving for ourselves and for no other, is still worth loving, is still worth fighting for.

This is our country — land of the morning sun, pearl of the orient seas, richly endowed with an untold wealth of resources. Our mountains are pregnant with rich minerals. Our mighty rivers hold the promise of power. Our fertile fields yield bountiful harvests. Our seas teem with the treasures of the deep. But the greatest wealth yet endowed upon our sun-kissed isles is our wonderful people — a vigorous, industrious people, easily given to laughter and the pursuit of simple pleasures.

Our people were the first in all Asia to declare our independence from western domination and the first to set up a democratic republic in this part of the world.

With Fervor Burning

Our government is the most stable in Southeast Asia. Never in our peacetime history has there been a military coup-d'etat, a change of government except by ballot, a dictatorship, forcible expropriation of property, riots, snake dances, or bloody purges. And we took care of our own Huks without importing mercenaries.

The Philippines has the second highest literacy rate in Asia (80 per cent compared to Malaysia's 47 per cent), second only to Japan (98 per cent) which has one of the highest in the world.

The Philippines has perhaps the largest ratio of students to population in the world: seven million students out of 30 million people or one out of every four.

We have the largest network of educational institutions in Southeast Asia: 23 universities, one reputed to be the largest in the world, another the oldest in Southeast Asia; and a total of 33,224 schools all over the country. So great is our pride in learning that almost every *nipa* hut sports a diploma at a place of honor.

The Philippines has the freest press in the world. Manila has 14 radio stations on the broadcast band and seven channels on the TV band. No other city in the world, not even Tokyo or New York, can claim as many radio and TV stations in their air lanes.

The Philippines is the only Christian country in Asia, where East meets West in a happy blending of cultures. It is the third largest English-speaking country in a world where English is the universal language.

We are one of the greatest exporters of skills in this part of the world, our doctors and nurses going as far as the United States and Europe, our engineers, technicians and musicians finding their way all over Asia and Oceania.

We are the largest exporter of coconut products, serving 65 per cent of the entire world's market (next is Indonesia serving only 15 per cent). We are the largest log exporters in the world (29 per cent of total world trade) and the second largest sugar exporter after Cuba. We serve 92.8 per cent of the world's market for abaca fiber.

We have third largest per capita income (P428) in the whole of Asia, the first being Japan, the second being Malaysia where the major portion of the national income mostly belongs to those other than the Malays.

Ours is the only country in the world that has succeeded in absorbing the Chinese. This is perhaps due to the Spaniards who, unlike the more liberal British and Dutch, persecuted the Chinese to such an extent that they had to seek conversion to Christianity and intermarry among the population, thus giving us our Bengsons, Sisons, Lichaucos, Tangcos, Chuidians, Tuasons, etc. and about 10 per cent of the bloodline of every one of us.

We have the most aggressive, the most freely competitive, and practically the only indigenous entrepreneurial class in Southeast Asia. Filipinos depend on no one to develop their country; our citizens have pioneered in all fields of endeavor, owning 86 per cent of all tangible wealth as per the latest tax census.

We have a population that cuts across class barriers, unlike any other in Asia. Almost every millionaire remembers his humble origins. Our rich and poor dress alike and mix without self-consciousness on every occasion.

And our women, ah, our women — they stand on the highest pedestal on earth. Ours is the only society in the world where the woman requires her man to pay the dowry and the wedding expenses, takes over the man's traditional role of keeper of the savings, risk-taker and entrepreneur, and invariably turns out to be the founder of the family fortune.

And no words, absolutely none, can express the joy and fierce pride that we Filipinos felt when Gemma Cruz, the nationalist daughter of a nationalist mother was adjudged as Miss International.

With Fervor Burning

Yes, let us count our blessings, thank the good Lord, and face our destiny without fear of tomorrow.

WHERE WENT OUR HERITAGE?

Thousand! of years ago, in three successive waves from Indonesia and Malaya, our intrepid forefathers swept across the heaving oceans to make their home in a group of emerald isles that has come to be known as the Philippines.

They organized themselves into tribal communities called barangays, each an independent economic unit producing for its own needs and wants. There was full employment, for each man, tilled his own land and operated a small home industry to supply his own tools, clothing and shelter. Gradually, these Malayan colonists traded with each other and with other lands. They traded with Arabs from the First century through the Shri-Visayan period up to the 12th century. They traded with the Chinese, who by the, 13th century, intermarried among the people, built sturdy houses, taught their families better ways of living, and brought in large quantities of ceramic ware still to be found in old village sites and ancient burial grounds.

When about the 14th century, the Philippines came under the sway of the Madjapahit Empire, our trade expanded throughout the Far East, reaching out to the old states of Cambodia, Champa, Siam, Tonkin, China and Japan. In an era uncomplicated by tariff barriers we were thus part of a Pan-Asian Common Market.

In the l6th century, the Spaniards came with the cross and the sword and took away from us our lands and our freedom. And for the next three hundred years, the Filipino was tied to the soil, a veritable feudal serf, under *encomenderos* and self-styled *ilustrados* who fattened on the fruits of his labor.

By royal fiat, Manila became just a little more than a way-station between China and the Mexican port of Acapulco. The Galleon Trade under Spanish monopoly consisted chiefly of silks, porcelain and other Chinese products, rather than Philippine products, until the early 19th century when more liberal policies were adopted and other foreigners, notably the British, were allowed to do business in the Philippines.

However, with the British acquisition of Singapore and Hongkong, and the opening of the Suez Canal in 1868, foreign commerce began rapidly to drift away from the Philippines.

Nevertheless, by the end of the 19th century, the Philippines had roads and a railroad that was second to none in all Asia. It had telephone and telegraph systems, and was the most westernized country in the whole of Asia. It was only a little later that Japan, in an impressive race to industrial supremacy, overtook the Philippines.

The Philippines, forced by its isolation from Spain to be self sufficient in its basic needs, spawned many native industries. And the wealth thus created was responsible for the birth of a class of Filipinos which was unique in the whole of Asia a cultured class which led the Revolution when the country became ready for it It was this elite class of Rizal and Aguinaldo that made the first successful attempt in Asia to shake off Western colonialism, and set up the first democratic republic in this part of the world.

We are tempted now to speculate on what might have been the economic destiny of the Philippines had the First Republic launched by General Aguinaldo on that fateful day of June 12, 1898, been allowed to take its course. Americans are prone, of course, to justify their colonial adventure by saying that the Philippines would have reverted back to the Dark Ages and would have been occupied by some other foreign power. It is my thesis that the Americans who say so are wrong.

When the Europeans came to America, they found primitive societies that could not project themselves from the impact of Western civilization. They came primarily to find new routes to the fabulous Orient, and later to found colonies for convicts and nonconformists. In doing so, they consigned the primitive Indians to extinction and made the continent their own.

But Europeans coming to Asia found civilizations in many respects superior to their own. They came, not to conquer primarily, but to trade. And they conquered only to impose law and order necessary to the conduct of trade.

Wherever local conditions were stable enough for trade, no conquest occurred. Thailand and Japan had strong central governments and were spared. China had enough of a central government even during the decadence of the Manchu Dynasty to prevent outright colonization. But the petty warring sultans of Indonesia and Malaya were no match for the vigor of Western traders bent on concessions and monopolies, always ready to back the more compliant sultan against his rivals and thus taking the effective power out of his hands. Had the Mogul Empire in India survived to the 19th century, there would have been no British Empire in India. The British conquest was largely a response to the collapse of local authority arising from the dissolution of the Mogul Empire and bitter trade rivalry with French traders.

The question that intrigues our minds is whether the Aguinaldo government of 1898 would have been stable enough to do business with, and thus preclude the necessity of conquest by other colonial powers.

Can there be any doubt that a people so united for 400 years under the Spanish crown, thoroughly Westernized and Christianized, heirs to the ancient cultures of Asia, and welded into a single nation by the common cause of freedom — a nation that declared its independence and established a democratic republic, the first in all of Asia — can there be any doubt that this island nation, like Japan, could have held off foreign intervention and developed into a modern commercial and industrial nation under the impetus of its own initiative?

WHITHER OUR DESTINY?

The Philippines was the very first among those that struggled under Western colonialism to achieve independence after World War II. Eighteen years have passed since then. During those years, many new nations have emerged, untroubled by self-doubts, purposeful in their march towards political and economic independence, taking their place, head erect as equals among the rest of the nations of the world.

And what have we done in the Philippines?

Before the Macapagal administration, we progressed a little, yes, but not to the limit of our potentialities. We have no Aswan High Dam, no Snowy Mountains Scheme, no Tata Steel Works, no Bandung Conference, no Common Market to mark the formative years after the birth of our nation. All those wasted years! — so fraught with uncertainty of purpose and direction, a traumatic fear of offending friends, a fatal hesitancy in the face of urgent opportunities and a tragic sense of being at cross-purposes with ourselves.

On a windswept sea, we were becalmed. We drifted aimlessly, while all around us tempestuous times responded to mighty movements and great purposes. While elsewhere in the world great loves and passions prevailed, we were rendered impotent by the guilt of an Oedipus complex that was leading us, as in the original

With Fervor Burning

Greek play, to shame and self-destruction.

Then came Diosdado Macapagal. Whatever else may be said of him, history will mark him down as the man who, as President, gave his country for the first time since independence, a renewed reason for being, a justification for its existence as a nation, in short, a national purpose.

With a remarkable sense of history, President Macapagal traced our continuing but "unfinished" revolution to achieve our national destiny — from its initial "military phase" led by Rizal, Bonifacio and Aguinaldo who gave our tribal peoples the unity of nationhood — through the "political phase" led by Quezon, Roxas and Osmena who gave the nation the reality of personal freedom and political independence — and at long last through the "economic phase" by which President Macapagal hopes to usher his people out of benighted centuries of poverty and social injustice into the light of day of economic independence, progress and prosperity.

History does not just happen. It is made. It is molded and willed into being by strength of mind and purpose. During the last two years of the Macapagal administration, we have witnessed great changes in the making:

— The first officially adopted Socio-Economic Program, a master blueprint for an all-out drive towards industrialization principally by Filipinos for Filipinos ("Filipino citizens shall be the chief beneficiaries as well as the principal determinants of our economic progress. We welcome all foreign assistance that does not wrest from us our supremacy over our own economic affairs");

— The passage of the Land Reform Code, outlawing for the first time the sharecropping system that had kept the mass of our population in virtual feudal serfdom for the last four centuries;

— The belated recognition of our true Independence Day, the revival of our historic claim to

With Fervor Burning

North Borneo, the historic Ecafe resolution that envisioned a regional Asian Common Market, the formation of Maphilindo, the revitalization of the Association of Southeast Asia, the firm assertion of the right of Asians to solve their Asian problems in the Asian way.

Blow after blow, like a monstrous dropforge, the will of one man is beating into shape the times to come.

Whither our destiny?

Let's focus our eyes up there where faith and prayers and visions have wing room.

We see the rise of a new and numerically preponderant middle class of factory owners, managers, industrial workers, professionals and intellectuals from the ranks of the poor and dispossessed, displacing the landed aristocracy and the parasitic class of colonial traders in the scheme of things.

We see the eventual industrialization and urbanization of our rural areas, as industries absorb surplus agricultural workers and finally bring about farm mechanization and the ultimate breakdown of medieval feudalism.

We see ourselves, in the flush of our Industrial Revolution, seeking new trade routes to larger consumer markets and greater sources of raw materials for our industries -- by joining Indonesia, Malaysia, Thailand and others in a Southeast Asian Common Market. Thus do we increase and diversify our export potentialities so that we do not depend on one market for a few raw material exports subject to the vagaries of world prices and power politics.

No longer will Southeast Asia be a quarreling conglomeration of Balkanized buffer states, but an effective economic bloc and eventually a political confederation of co-equal states, a counterweight to the great nations of Japan, China, India and White Australia.

With Fervor Burning

As the most experienced, most literate, most politically stable, most technologically advanced and most industrialized nation in Southeast Asia, we shall find international power and influence gravitating to our universities, our political institutions, and our industrial complexes.

And finally with the onrush of the tides of time, we shall see our own native land, no longer a mere show window in the Far East, separated from its neighbors by the glass barrier of colonial double-allegiance, but a hustling and bustling market place for all Asia, a leader among nations dedicated to the proposition that in spite of differences in race, religion, culture or politics, man unto his fellow man can be a friend forever.

Such then is our dream. Perhaps not in the next decade will it come true. Not yet but soon, sooner than we expect, "God will walk on brown legs."

As a Filipino poet turned businessman once wrote:

Not yet, not yet Sleep not in peace;
There are a thousand waters to be spanned;
There are a thousand bridges to be crossed;
There are a thousand crosses to be borne.
The glory hour will come!
Out of the silent dreaming, from the seven thousand fold silence,
We shall emerge, saying:
WE ARE FILIPINOS
And no longer be ashamed.

RIZAL'S DREAM COMES TRUE

In Rizal's novel, *El Filibusterismo*, the young hero Isagani was asking his sweetheart Paulita to come to his hometown. Paulita was shy about accepting the invitation, as shy as most girls are when invited to a provincial joyride without a chaperone.

Paulita politely refused, indirectly of course, by imposing an impossible condition. Since there was no railroad at the time, Paulita declared she would only travel by train. Isagani, never to lose hope, answered, "Within a short time, there will be a railroad."

"When?" Paulita teased. "When I am an old woman?"

Then follows one of the most prophetic of Rizal's passages. Isagani unburdens his dream:

"Ah, you do not know what we can do in a few years. You do not realize the energy and enthusiasm that are awakening in the country after the sleep of the centuries. Our young men are working day and night dedicating to the fatherland all their intelligence, all their time, all their strength.

"Tomorrow, we shall be citizens of the Philippines, whose destiny will be a glorious one, because it will be in loving hands. Ah yes, the future is ours.

"I see life stirring in these regions so long dead and lethargic. I see towns rise along the railroads. I see factories everywhere. I hear steam hiss, engines rattle! I see smoke rise — their heavy breathing. I smell the oil — the sweat of monsters at incessant toil.

"This port, this river where commerce is in its death agony, we shall see full of ships from other nations. This pure air and these stones now so clean will be crowded with boxesand barrels, the products of human industry. But let it not matter, for we shall have comfortable coaches to takeus far into the interior, seeking other breezes   still fresh, other scenes still unstained, on other shore still untouched, wrapping us in coolness upon the slopes of the mountains.

"Free from the system of exploitation, without hatred or distrust, the people will labor because then, labor will cease to be a despicable thing, it will no longer be servility imposed upon a slave. With steady eyes, unafraid, we shall extend our hands to one another; and commerce, industry, agriculture, the sciences, will develop under the mantle of liberty, with wise and just laws, as in prosperous England."

Paulita smiled dubiously, shook her head, sighed and said, "Dreams, dreams, dreams."

Such was the dream of Isagani. Such was the dream of the man who created Isagani, the man we call "the greatest man the Malay Race ever produced," our national hero, Dr. Jose Rizal.

More than seventy years ago, beyond the medieval scene of tyranny, feudalism and oppression, Rizal envisioned a free and democratic Philippines grown great through nationalism and industrialization.

Today, we see factories everywhere, dotting the landscape where once were rice fields, making almost every article of common use — from ships to floor wax, from soap to nuts and bolts. We see ships of many nations call at our ports to discharge raw materials for our industries and to load up on export products for other shores.

Today we see the rise of an industrial middle class made up of factory owners, financiers, professionals of all types and industrial workers for whom "labor is no longer a despicable thing," displacing the feudal lords of the *encomienda*. Labor unions and progressive management guarantee that "labor shall no longer be servility imposed upon a slave."

Today in spite of Goldwaterite attempts to reduce us back to the pastoral peace of the plantation and dependence on foreign import-export trading posts, we have come to see "commerce, industry, agriculture, the sciences, develop as in prosperous England" — prosperous England where by deliberate statecraft and economic protectionism, the first Industrial Revolution was brought into being.

And thanks to Claro M. Recto, one of the greatest Filipinos in our tide of times, a resurgent nationalism is bringing this country back into the care of loving hands . . . not the clenched fists of communists, not the itchy palms of carpet-baggers . . . but the "loving hands" of Filipino patriots and nationalists.

Thus Rizal the dreamer dreamed. And elsewhere in his novel, probably with a premonition of what subsequently came to pass on a bleak December mom, he wrote for those of us who are now seeing his dream come true:

"I die before I see the dawn break upon my fatherland. You who shall see that dawn — salute it And be not forgetful of those who fell in the night."

WHERE ARE THE YOUTH?

Where are the youth who will consecrate their golden hours, their illusions, and their enthusiasm to the welfare of their native land?

Where are the youth who will generously pour out their blood to wash away so much shame, so much crime, so much abomination?

Where are you, youth, who will embody in yourselves the vigor of life that has left our veins, the purity of ideas that has been contaminated in our minds, the fire of enthusiasm that has been quenched in our hearts?

We await you, O youth! Come, we await you!

— DR. JOSE RIZAL

With Fervor Burning

* * *

Always, when the time comes forthe doing and the dying, the youth of the land are the ones called upon to take up the challenge.

The youth all over the world have always been the instrument of change and progress. Young, physically strong, minds   receptive   to new   ideas, hearts that throb with compassion and idealism, free from everyday responsibilities, free to think and to act, impatient   and   reckless   —   the   youth   have always led the mass movements that pushed humanity toward new frontiers.

We who are no longer young tend to be more cautious, more conservative, more afraid of change. Perhaps because we are no longer strong enough to withstand the rigors of conflict. Perhaps because the immediate problem of raising a family and providing security for the future, make us fear the reaction of those upon whom we depend for a living and blur our vision of new horizons. And we who are no longer young are, more often than not, inclined to counsel the youth on prudence, caution, discretion, submission, and the acceptance of the status quo.

In Rizal's *"El Filibusterismo"*, we witness a typical scene between an old man and a youth. The old lawyer, Senor Pasta, was listening to the young student, Isagani, expounding on the problems of Spanish colonial policies in the Philippines, the tyranny and corruption, and the need for change.

Senor Pasta waved his handas if to dispel the ideas suggested and exclaimed, "Dreams, illusions, fancies!"

The old man   placed   his   hand affectionately on young Isagani's shoulder and said,"I amgoing to give you one advice, because I see that you are intelligent and the advice will not be wasted.

"You're going to study medicine? Well confine yourself of learning how to put on plasters and apply ointments; and don't try to improve or impair the condition of your people.

"Always remember that charity begins at home, for man should not seek on this earth any more than the greatest amount of happiness for himself. If you chase windmills like Don Quixote, you will have no career, nor will you ever amount to anything. All will abandon you; your own countrymen will be the first to laugh at you. Believe me, you will remember how right I am, whenyou have gray hairs like I have, gray hairs such as these!"

As the old lawyer stroked hisscanty gray hair, and smiled sadly, Isagani replied with equalsadness:

"When I have gray hairs such as yours, sir, and turn my gaze back over my past and see that I have worked only for myself, without having done what I plainly could and should have done for the country that has given me birth, for the people who share my life and my love — then sir, every gray hair will be a thorn, and will turn white with shame!"

How many times has this scene been played — in the lifetime of every single one of us — in our homes with our parents, in our schools with our teachers, in our offices with our employers, in the higher councils of state with the powers-that-be?

Yet the youth of the land were always there, in the moment of their country's greatest need, just where they had to be to best serve her.

It was the generation of Rizal, Bonifacio and Aguinaldo, young men hardly out of their twenties, who spearheaded the Propaganda Movement against Spain and began the armed struggle that was to be the first setback of Western colonialism in all of Asia.

A generation later, Quezon, Osmena and Recto all young men below the age of 30 — took up the parliamentary struggle that gave us our political independence. It was the time of self-confident nationalism, when one could exclaim without being accused as a subversive: "Better a government run like hell by Filipinos than a government run like heaven by the Americans."

Years later, a group called the Young Philippines which included Wenceslao Vinzons, Arturo Tolentino and Diosdado Macapagal, rallied around the causes of Social Justice and "Malaya Irredenta" that presaged the historic passsage of the Land Reform Code and the formation of ASA and Maphilindo. It was the time when no political leader could run for public office without presenting himself and his platform before the scrutiny of the students of the University of the Philippines and others.

Today, as a youthful nation, and most uniquely, as a nation of youths — 72 percent of our population are of ages 29 years and below, 56 percent are of 19 years and below the Philippines has yet to produce a single youth leader of heroic proportions.

In a nation corrupted by war and "liberation," still clinging to its fleshpots, sacred cows and brazen idols — in a nation not quite yet a nation, awaiting the final triumph of an Unfinished Revolution that holds the promise of economic independence and national dignity — in such a nation, surely there must be some young men somewhere, sickened and outraged by our times, who will rise to take up the challenge of this generation.

I am Youth.

I am he who dreams, but who shall make your dreams come true.

I am he who shall take the green of your pastures, the gold of your hills, the might of your rivers — fashion them with my hands, my heart, my mind, and transform them into life and power!

I am he who shall take this nation which you will someday bequeath to me — breaths into it the warmth of my ideals — build it firm and strong and higher up to the stars, till the universe shall know of its strength!

I am he who shall think, work, act — until the

With Fervor Burning

Filipino Tao, ill starred and striped no longer in the prison garb of self doubt and double allegiance, shall stand head high in pride and dignity, on every field and valley of this land!

> *I am a laborer. I am a builder. I am a dreamer. I am Youth.*
> *Heed me — for the future is mine!*

> *(— Paraphrased with the author's permission from a school oration (1940) by a very young Ateneo student named Raul S. Manglapus.)*

THE GRAND ILLUSION

National glory is a theatrical concept. In the task of nation-building, renovating a stagnant society, preserving a way of life in the face of imminent danger, or fulfilling a mission to change the world — there is a need for self-sacrifice and united action that can only be brought about if the people are given the grand illusion that they are participating as heroes in some colossal spectacle.

We speak of the "theater" of war and battle "scenes." Great generals never fail to remind their soldiers "that the eyes of the world are upon them, that their ancestors are watching them and that posterity shall hear them." In front of such an audience, self-sacrifice is robbed of its inconvenience and becomes a magnificent theatrical gesture.

Hitler cast his people in the role of redeemers of a brutalized nation and marched them goose-stepping in brown shirts toward the glory of a thousand-year Reich. The Communists see themselves as the wave of the future moving inexorably toward the horizons of a classless society.

The present-day Israelis, Egyptians, Chinese, and even French see themselves as ancient people reviving memories of a glorious past and led by visions of a breathtaking future.

The Indians assume the Christ-like posture of Gandhi in a world gone mad with nuclear brinkmanship. The Japanese assume an aggressive role as Asia's hope in a white-dominated world economy. The Indonesians cast themselves as beleaguered heroes in the fight against colonialism.

In their finest hour, the British played their heroic roles before a vast audience of generations past, present and future (conjured up for them by Churchill) upon a stage lighted by a burning city to the music of roaring guns and screaming bombs.

What kind of role does the white man play among the colored races of the world? Wherever the locale happens to be Kipling's India, Tarzan's Africa, William Holden's South-east Asia or even the Wild West of the red Indians — the white man plays the same role in what has come to be known as the "Great Hollywood Drama," familiar to anybody exposed to movies and television.

What is the plot of the Great Hollywood Drama?

The wicked white man (or a native despot) rides herd over the helpless and frightened natives. The good white man comes into the scene, and in a climactic struggle, triumphs over the evil man. And the natives hail the good white man as their saviour.

The plot oftentimes vary from this standard fare. The frightened natives, goaded to desperate action, rise up in arms and threaten to obliterate their oppressors. The good white man, apparently appalled by this usurpation of his anointed role, tries to stop the impending battle. He fails, and the plot sickens. Does he help in the natives' cause? You bet your silver spurs, he does not Sadly, reluctantly, the good white man rides forth to join the beleaguered white community, now surrounded by the avenging, thundering herd of native savages. And guess who wins in the end? The white men, of course.

The moral of the Great Hollywood Drama, it seems, is that the poor natives are ill-advised to rely on their own initiative and resources, but must wait patiently for some blonde, blue-eyed hero to act as their champion and redeemer...or else.

Nobody, of course, should take Hollywood to task for this nonsense. It is as idiotic as the "grand illusions" of Hitler or the communists, but we must admit that this type of make-believe has inspired the white man to take up the white man's burden, civilize the savages and make the world safe for their democracy.

What is so tragic is that we Filipinos have no grand illusion of our own. We do not generally think of ourselves as the main characters in the great saga of nation-building. Instead, by constant exposure to movies, we have brainwashed ourselves into being supporting players and extras in the Great Hollywood Drama, whose script gives us no better role than that of Gunga Din, Sabu the Elephant Boy or Ton to the Indian sidekick.

Thus the story of the last war, in reality one of the most glorious in our history, is depicted on our movie screens as the adventure of an All-American team with Filipino mascots who chatter unintelligibly in the background like the Japs. And endless rhetoric is spouted to make us eternally grateful to America for liberation and veteran's benefits.

Our national pride might have been better served if we recall that as American nationals owing allegiance to the President of the United States, we did fight for American and not vice-versa; that we did most of the fighting in the Philippines to save Australia and set the stage for America's recovery and return; and that, by God, we have a right to expect America to be grateful to us, and not vice versa.

Also, in the conduct of our economic affairs, we

have a tendency to give much more than due credit to foreign experts, foreign aid and foreign investments for most of the progress which we ourselves have accomplished. It was Pilipino capital that pioneered in most of the industries that ushered in our Industrial Revolution, in spite of foreign advisers who kept reminding us that we are "basically an agricultural country." By the last Tax Census, Filipinos contributed 86%, Chinese immigrants 12% and foreigners only 2% of all the investments in this country.

But break our hearts, for we must swallow our pride and hail the blonde blue-eyed hero as our saviour and redeemer as per the script of the Great Hollywood Drama which has been to us, not a grand illusion calling for greatness, but a sad mad delusion leading our nation inexorably to the ash-heap of oblivion.

EACH HAS HIS LONELY BATTLE

She came back to her hometown which had not changed much since she left it 20 years ago. She came back, now a rich widow with vengeance in her heart and she offered the town and all its people a huge fortune on one condition: that they take the life of the man who wronged her.

She took over the factories and the mines, the source of livelihood of the people, and kept them idle. She brought in refrigerators, TV sets, cars, and all the good things in life and gave them away on credit, confident that the people would indeed take up her proposition to be able to afford paying her back.

In the final scene, the townspeople gathered in the public square where after the mockery of a trial, they condemned the man to death. The woman stood up and spoke with venomous contempt:

"Is there any one here who would now stand up for this man, and say that this is an injustice? Not one? Not even one?

"Twenty years ago, I was made pregnant by a man who did not want to marry me. For the price of a bottle of brandy, two other man swore in court that I was a prostitute. I was beaten up, my baby taken from me. And as I was sent away in disgrace on a cold night, the only one who gave me attention was the constable and he did it with a kick. And all the while, I cried out in anguish — is there no one here to help me? Not one? Not even one?

"Keep your 30 pieces of silver. But let this condemned man live. Let him walk among you for the rest of his life — to remind himself and all of you of the vileness and poverty of your own souls!"

This is the story of the movie "The Visit" recently shown in a downtown theater. One left the theater with an eerie feeling of involvement in the sins of our contemporary society.

A few years ago a man named Moises Padilla was beaten and tortured by a gang of political goons, dragged from town to town at the end of a rope and finally murdered. Of the hundreds of people who witnessed this public display of cruelty and madness, not one came forward to stop it.

An American *mestiza* was forcibly abducted in full view of a crowd of people, none of whom lifted a finger in her behalf.

"Let Recto do it!" cried Carmen Guerrero Nakpil bitterly. "And let us give him a big hand afterwards. Admiration does not cost a centavo. Applause never hurt anyone. We appreciated what he did, don't we? But while he was doing all that, how comfortable, cozy, and cowardly were all the little dark corners into which we crawled."

The world of the Filipino businessman is a

lonely, fearful world where he must expect little support from his own countrymen, and no quarter from the extraneous forces that would consign him to the status of a second class citizen in his own country.

When the textile manufacturers were protesting against the unfair dumping of foreign textiles into the market, was there anyone who gave them public support? Certainly not the flour millers. But the time came for the flour millers to suffer the dumping of white Australian flour into their market, and no one else spoke up for them. Not the steel mills anyway. Then inevitably in their own turn, the steel mills found themselves at the mercy of foreign companies dumping steel bars into the Philippine market And they too stood alone.

One student of the contemporary scene is quoted by Ralph Tagle:"The cosmopolitan cocktail circle is the sacrificial site for the good name of the Filipino people. Many a foreigner or his agent, it seems, feels free to make sweeping judgments on the intelligence and integrity of any Filipino not within earshot — from the President of the Philippines, through politicians, government officials, businessmen, columnists, labor leaders, employees, down to the thieving houseboy at home. And all Filipinos within earshot join in this unholy ritual so as 'not to offend the guests,' without knowing that sooner or later when their back is turned, it will be their turn to be the sacrificial lamb."

To be a Filipino nowadays is to be alone. Each fights his lonely battle for personal survival. No one joins another to fight the total war for the survival of the nation.

Indeed after 18 years of independence, can we really call ourselves a nation? When will we learn that nationalism is the sense of belonging to each other; that when one of us dies, everyone else dies a little and the bells toll for the rest of us?

If it meant risking personal safety or that of loved

ones — if it meant the possible loss of a scholarship or a travel grant, a fat retainer's fee or a well-paying job. a good business deal or a political campaign contribution — or if it just meant "kicking" an ingrained addiction to colonial double-allegiance or offending the sensibilities of guests — would anyone stand up and denounce an injustice done to a brother Filipino?

Not one? Not even one?

Someday some of us will take our turn at the rack. A man is beaten and dragged through streets. A politician or a writer or a labor leader hears his name bandied around in whispers as a leftist, a foreign agent, a libertine, an opportunist. A businessman finds his whole life's work crushed under the sheer weight of unfair foreign competition. An employee is fired and black-balled because he feels he should be a Filipino above all else. A student or a professor is dragged before an investigating committee for expressing views outside of the classroom.

Some of us in turn will get spied upon, maligned, deprived of livelihood, threatened, bullied, harmed, and we too will know, as Moises Padilla did, as Recto did, what it really means to be a Filipino in the Philippines — a patriot without a country, a nationalist without a nation, crying out with all the pain and anguish of the loneliest man on earth:

"Is there no one here to help? Not one? Not even one?"

ALIENATION OF THE INTELLECTUALS
(or Eggheads Strengthen Political Parties)

We Filipinos have always felt a degree of affinity with the Democratic Party of the United States. For it was under Democratic administrations that we were definitely promised and finally granted the restoration of the Independence we won and lost in 1898 *et sequitur.* And our touching faith in America was mostly inspired by Woodrow Wilson's idealism, Roosevelt's social conscience and Kennedy's liberalism.

The Republicans, on the other hand, had actively espoused America's Manifest Destiny which envisioned the Philippines as an outpost of American colonial traders. The Republican Party of U.S. Big Business has been associated in our minds, not only with imperialism, but also isolationism, McCarthyism, brinkmanship and the Goldwater brand of unfettered free enterprise that has spawned robber barons and great depressions.

Our minds should be at ease. According to Mr. George Gallup, the Republic Party of McKinley, Harding, Hoover, McCarthy and Goldwater has been consistently on the decline in American party politics for the past quarter of a century. In 1940, 38 per cent of American adults considered themselves Republicans; in 1964, only 25 per cent did so.

The decline of the Republican Party and its disastrous defeat in the last American elections is attributed to its "alienation of intellectuals" — a valuable lesson to our politicians and political parties here in the Philippines.

Walter Lippmann in the November 23rd issue of Newsweek Magazine convincingly develops this thesis, thus in his own words:

"Because the Republican leadership has been so wrong on the great problems of American public life — on the issue of war and peace (isolationism and McCarthyism at home, imperialism and brinkmanship abroad), on the issues of economic progress and social welfare (Smithsonian free enterprise of the robber baron variety) — it has repelled the best brains of the oncoming generation.

The Democrats, on the contrary, under Wilson,

under Franklin Roosevelt, and under Kennedy, have sought out and wooed and provided attractive careers for the talented.

It is no accident that the Democratic Party has been overwhelmingly stronger than the Republican in the colleges, among scientists and scholars and artists, among the intellectual communities in the cities. (The Republicans on the other hand, count as their supporters Big Business and the top brass of the armed forces.)

The Democratic Party wanted the eggheads, not because they have many votes, but because they have influence and ideas and from these eggheads the Democratic Party has drawn enormous strength. From these eggheads, which Roosevelt, Kennedy and Johnson gathered around them came the ideas and programs around which were built the Democratic majorities.

The highly educated, the specialists, and the experts are in numbers a tiny minority. But their influence on the formation of public opinion, even more on the invention and making of policy, is incalculable.

Thus, modem fiscal policy has produced the good times which have made President Johnson virtually unbeatable. The germ of the ideas for that policy was fertilized in the brains of theorists, one a Swede (Gunmar Myrdal) and the other an Englishman (Lord Maynard Keynes). The present generation of American economists has beep applying and developing this discovery and is in the process of proving by experiment that it works.

This commanding position in the field of ideas has in the past half-century given the Democrats a virtual monopoly of constructive proposals in public affairs. That is why there is a certain truth in the Goldwater complaint that the liberal and progressive Republicans are "me-too"-ists. The Democrats have pre-empted almost all the attractive proposals because they have included so much of the intellectual community which is capable of devising attractive proposals.

Ever since Wilson and Roosevelt, the central Republican leadership has been alienated from the intellectual community, and in the years when it backed McCarthy (and his Communist witch-hunt), it in effect declared war on the intellectual community.

The Republican Party will not, I believe, restore itself as long as it cuts itself off from the bright young men who carry in their heads the seed com of the future.

The Republicans will have to find a way to end their alienation from the best brains of the nation. It is this alienation which expressed itself as 'he never met a payroll,' he has long hair, too high a brow, or he is sinister and subversive.

This alienation is the root of the decline of the Republican Party."

Thus we quote Walter Lippmann (the words between parenthesis are ours, however), one of the greatest end most durable of American political commentators.

Goldwater and the "dangerous fringe" that he represented has been thoroughly discredited and repudiated by the vast majority of the American people.

But what should cause us grave concern is that two out of every three Americans residing in the Philippines have expressed, according to a recent poll, a preference for Goldwater and his policies during the last American elections. The present U.S. Ambassador William McCormick Blair is a respected Democrat who had been long associated with Adlai Stevenson and John F. Kennedy, the greatest liberal and intellectual leaders of their times.

When he appealed for sobriety and understanding in Philippine-American relations during his speech before the Rotary, it can only be presumed that he was appealing not only to hypersensitive Filipino nationalists, but also to local Super-Americans, McCarthyists, John Birchers, and robber-baronic free enterprisers of the Goldwater stripe — who brand President Macapagal's socio-economic program and our social welfare legislations as dangerously socialistic — who rant and rave against legitimate national aspirations as communist-inspired who regard our sincere efforts to promote industrialization and a Filipino middleclass as an attempt to create an oligarchy to challenge their oligarchy — who are alienating Filipino intellectuals and entrepreneurs and doing irreparable harm to the great American nation we love so well.

INVESTMENT (FOREIGN) TYPES

At one time or smother, most of us get invited to the inauguration of some big factory. A guide is assigned to show us the wonders of industrial progress. We are subjected to the exhilirating sight of iron monsters hard at work, sweating oil, and regurgitating the products of human industry. We see tall chimneys pointing upward to the heavens, and factory smoke rising to challenge the accredited clouds of the sky. We see handsomely clad Filipino workers watching the dance of the dials and pulling levers with precise and punctual hands. And when the time comes for the speeches and the toasts, we are told that all these are the result of something called "foreign investment" whose anointed task it is to dignify Filipino labor, to raise the standard of living of the masses, and to provide them with the blessings of civilization, democracy and freedom, otherwise denied them by the extremes of nationalism and the oligarchy of Filipino vested interests.

With Fervor Burning

All over the world the homage to foreign investment has developed into a cult. Foreign investment is the answer to all social problems, the universal cure to all economic ills. Is it, really? Is it a miracle cure like penicillin or a patent medicine like Uncle Ebenezer's Liver Pills?

Our personal opinion is that foreign investment is neither a miracle cure nor a patent medicine. It is a shelf of many different remedies, of varying potencies and varied side effects.

"Foreign Investment" is a catch-all term for (1) foreign grants-in-aid, (2) foreign loans, (3) immigrant capital, and (4) direct investments. Direct investments are in turn classified into (a) joint ventures and (b) those fully owned by foreigners; and are either (a) invited capital or (b) colonial investments.

Foreign grants-in-aid are gifts by foreign governments or international agencies as an investment to gain the goodwill of the host country. The US Agency For International Development (AID) for instance has given our country in direct grants some $3.8 million this year. Under the United Nations Technological Assistance Program, we received some $8.5 million this year. The Philippine government gave South Vietnam $1 million medical and technological assistance. The Japanese gave us in Reparations payments some $25 million a year, in expiation for World War II.

Repayable foreign loans are usually given for self-liquidating projects by the World Bank, the Export-Import Bank and other similar institutions. Recently we received $623 million for an integrated steel mill project, $10 million for the purchase of interisland ships and some $23 million in low-interest long-term AID loans for development projects.

Immigrant capital, not only in cash but also in skills, are brought in by foreigners who eventually become citizens of the host country. Outstanding examples are Col. Hans Menzi, and Earl Carroll (in

1974, we are assured). There is another word to describe those who come in with nothing but a carpet bag.

Direct investments in joint venture with Filipino citizens have been actively encouraged by the Macapagal administration. The last few years have seen the establishment of joint ventures by General Electric, Rohm & Haas, Shell Oil Co., Reynolds Metals, American Standard Fixtures, and many others.

An example of a fully owned foreign subsidiary is Esso (Philippines) Inc., which is owned and controlled by the Standard Oil of New Jersey. Some foreign subsidiaries were specifically invited into the Philippines, such as Dole Pineapple and Esso Fertilizer. Some were not invited; they entered the country during the bygone colonial period and prospered under conditions unilaterally imposed on the host country.

In other parts of Africa and Asia, some colonial investments proved to be a problem to the host country, for they repatriate their original capital many times over in a constant drain of the country's resources, are savagely intent on retaining their extra-territorial privileges and have grown powerful enough to apply political, economic and even military pressures on the host country. One can only cite United Fruit Co. in Latin America, Suez Canal Co. in Egypt, Union Miniere in the Congo and certain oil companies that always seem to be involved in the affairs of the Middle East.

Fortunately, in the Philippines there are few such colonial investments, and most of them behave as proper guests in this country. Most of the oil companies which are the objects of criticism in other countries are held high in the esteem of Filipinos. Shell Oil Co. and Gulf Oil in particular pioneered in joint ventures with Filipinos; Tidewater, Caltex and Mobil Oil mind their own business well and are appreciated for their civic spirit, beauty contests and arty magazines. These companies do not indulge in spreading vicious rumors along the cocktail circuit about the personal habits of our government officials and columnists, nor presume to make sweeping judgments on their intelligence and integrity, nor corrupt them, nor threaten them with loss of livelihood, nor finance them to fight each other, nor conspire with them against national interest. We are indeed lucky that most such foreign investors have responded graciously to our hospitality and forbearance.

It is no wonder that we in the Philippines, unlike most of our brother Asians, welcome foreign investments to supplement (but of course, not to supplant) domestic capital in the development of our country.

INVESTMENTS AND U.S. GROWTH

One of the many statements advanced by members of the American Chamber of Commerce is that the United States, a former colony like the Philippines, attained the status of a colossus through Foreign Investment.

Indeed this is a gospel truth.

As the Philippines was a colony of Spain and the United States, so was the US a colony of Great Britain. But the difference ends there. Unlike Filipinos, the forebears of present-day Americana were the colonizers, not the colonized. They never knew what it was to be debased and brutalized because of the color of their skin, and no such traumatic experience ever gave them a colonial mentality such as afflicts present-day Filipinos. They were British subjects under the protection of the British crown; and they brought with them to America the British traditions of fair play, justice and the judgment of one's peers, as well as personal freedom and the sanctity of one's home. When they revolted against Great Britain, they did so on nothing more than the issue of "taxation without representation.'

Except for the red Indians, every American is either a foreigner or a descendant of a foreigner. Therefore, every investment they made in the United States is a foreign investment.

Theirs is what is known as immigrant capital, probably the greatest factor in the growth of the colossus that is America today.

No less important were the foreign loans which helped build up America in its first century of growth.

A pamphlet entitled "The Role of Foreign Investment in US Economic Growth" by Professor Wilson Schmidt of George Washington University tells the whole story.

* * *

The United States was blessed with "massive immigration of skilled and knowledgeable people who brought. .. new techniques of production. .. bringing capital with them — an average of $75 per head." They came with a little more than hope in their hearts, knowledge in their minds and skill in their hands. They came — DuPont, Carnegie and others — and became part of America itself. And it is they who made America great For the wealth of any country is measured by the skills, the energy and the character of its people.

The great firm of E.I. du Pont de Nemours & Co. was started by a member of the du Pont family who, frightened out of France by the revolution, stayed in America to engage in the manufacture of gunpowder. With the help of loans from France, he launched a firm which was to make the gunpowder that powered the pioneer's hunting rifle, blasted stumps and boulders to make farmlands out of the wilderness, preserved America's independence in the second war against the British (1812), and helped maintain the Union during the Civil War. It blasted out the paths for roads, canals and rails to unify America economically and went on to promote "better living through chemistry."

There is a price to pay for immigrant capital, and the price is the painful process of integrating the immigrant into the body politic. The process sometimes involves intolerance, discrimination and even outright persecution. The body politic, like the human body, will, in the natural course of things, excrete a foreign body it cannot absorb. Thus, even in the United States, there had been outbursts of discrimination and violence at every successive wave of immigrant Jews, Chinese, Irish, Italians and, even today, the Puerto Ricans.

"The United States received only a small proportion of its total inflow of foreign capital through foreign owned enterprises.. foreigners chiefly bought bonds rather than stocks...."

* * *

Thus the greatest single source of foreign funds for the development of the United States is foreign loans.

At the start of America's first century of growth, the nation borrowed from foreigners a sum equal to 14 per cent of all reproducible and tangible wealth in the United States. Foreign loans, specially from France, financed one-fifteenth of the cost of the American Revolution.

Foreign loans financed the Erie Canal which opened the West to the Atlantic ports. Foreign loans financed the growth of such cities as Washington, D.C., Boston, New York.

Foreignloans financedthe Louisiana Purchase which doubled the territory of the nation and paved the way towards its expansion to the Pacific Ocean. Foreign loans financed the tremendous growth of American railroads which spanned the continent and opened up the development of the West.

But it must be emphasized that these foreign loans did not involve foreign control and management, except when due and in default. Even JP. Morgan who represented British bondholders, by taking over the rights of unpaid creditors, acquired enough resources to bail out the US government in some of its greatest economic crises.

These foreign loans were repayable, but it took the United States about 140 years to repay them. It was only after the first World War when America financed the war-impoverished European nations, that the United States was able to liquidate its foreign loans, and became itself a creditor nation.

As a creditor nation, Mother America is now seeking to do for others what others have done for her; she is now exporting her own brand of foreign investment at the rate of four thousand million dollars a year. American investors have today assets abroad of roughly 35 thousand million dollars.

This brand of foreign investment is not immigrant capital, not so much foreign loans, but what is known as "foreign owned direct investment" which we welcome into the Philippines in joint venture with Filipino citizens, especially in areas of endeavor where Filipinos are unwilling or unable to invest.

GREAT DEBATE ON ECONOMY

For the last ten years, our national efforts were wasted in local politicking, graft and corruption, economic mendicancy and slavish adherence to another nation's foreign policy. Even as our industrialists launched this country almost against its will into a belated Industrial Revolution, the great Economic Debate raged on between the landowner-importer-exporter group on one hand, and the industrialists, the professionals and the labor leaders on the other. The issues were clear: an agricultural economy based on domestic consumption? *Laissez faire* to perpetuate a colonial status quo, or a planned economy to promote industrialization?

For the last 10 years, the great debate raged between the landed aristocracy on one hand and the industrial middle class on the other. But the rest of the Filipino people had a hard time choosing sides. The vague, vast and complex economic theories defied simple understanding. And confusion reigned among the ranks of the combatants, among landlords who were also industrialists and industrialists who were also importers. Our political leaders, who were mostly lawyers on retainer from both sides, came up with an ineffective compromise in the form of something called a "balanced agro-industrial program" which meant absolutely nothing because nobody knew where the fulcrum of the balance is supposed to be. As a result, our economic efforts in Bygone years have been fraught with uncertainty of purpose and direction, a tendency to mendicancy, a fatal hesitancy in the face of urgent necessities, and a sense of being at cross-purposes with ourselves.

Today, we have reason to look to the future with much more than hope. For the President, through his five-year socio-economic program, has finally settled the 10-year Great Economic Debate. President Macapagal envisions a rising economic growth primarily through industrialization, and the development of our material and labor resources, not by raw material exports, but by a whole complex of basic and inter-mediate industries geared to produce materials for our consumption goods industries.

The shift from consumption goods industries to more basic industries requires much more capital investment than heretofore needed for every peso increase in output and for every new laborer employed.

With Fervor Burning

His immediate target is to mobilize gross domestic savings to achieve new capital formation of P12.7 billion over five years. With this capital, he hopes to maintain the rate of growth in gross domestic product at 6 per cent compounded every year up to 1967. This is the same rate of growth that prevailed during the period of controls. This, he hopes, is enough to restore economic stability, alleviate the plight of the common man and establish a dynamic self-sustaining basis for future growth. Translated into action, his program envisions specific provisions for moral regeneration, self-sufficiency in food, tariff protection for local industries, incentives for foreign investment, essential government services to promote production, selective export tax on certain protected exports and on processible raw materials, repeal of the margin fee and barter law, anti-smuggling measures and a revision of the tax structure.

As Macapagal envisioned it, free enterprise does not mean a relapse into laissez faire where dog eats dog, the devil takes the hindmost and the law of the jungle prevails. He did not abdicate the responsibility of the government for the nation's economic development. It is clear from his program that while eschewing direct and arbitrary control over private enterprise, he is prepared to use his powers to intervene in and guide the forces of the market to direct and accelerate economic growth along desired channels.

Above all, he called for self-sacrifice, self-discipline and simple living on the part of the people who elected him into office. President Macapagal has charted his course through the burning desert towards the promised land. The people will follow him, as follow him they must. But the next few years will tell whether he is Moses brooding alone at the edge of the desert, or Joshua leading them on to the promised land.

WE WANT CHANGE NOW

We have a dream. Our dream is to see the Philippines rise as an independent, prosperous and democratic nation, grown great through industrialization and nationalism.

To achieve this, we don't want stability; we do not want equilibrium, balance or established order; we do not want the perpetuation of the status quo; we want change, and we want change now.

First of all, we want to get rid of the feudal type of import-export plantation economy that has impoverished our people for milleniums past and submitted them to the domination of a landed aristocracy and a parasitic group of foreign adventurers.

We reject the pastoral peace of our grandfathers as a permanent way of life. For as hunting gave way to the farm pasture, primitive agriculture must give way to mechanized farming and industrialization. Industry is the only economic activity that keeps pace with population growth. Industry begets other industries in geometric progression in the same way that man begets children, and the resultant increase in job opportunities will absorb the surplus agricultural workers out of the farms, and pave the way for eventual farm mechanization.

History is witness to this. In the United States, only 11% of the labor population work in the farms, yet they grow enough food to feed not only the entire United States but the free world as well, and still have enough left over to plow under. In the Philippines, 65% of our population live in the farms, where all we have to do is to flick a seed into the ground to make it grow, and we cannot even grow enough to feed ourselves.

Industrialization then is the answer. But industrialization cannot be pursued without sacrifice, sacrifice to limit consumption expenditures in order to acquire capital equipment, sacrifice to accept temporary disadvantages for lasting gain. Such sacrifice can only be borne by a people conscious of their identity and continuity as a nation, a people with a sense of common destiny, in short, a people imbued with Nationalism, that creative conceit which makes the impossible possible.

This nationalism, this creative conceit, is incompatible with the alien-induced notion that we Filipinos can never progress without foreign aid, without foreign investment, without foreign bases, without the colonial mentality of a Gunga Din or Sabu the Elephant Boy and their cloying obeisance to the Great White Father.

Industrialization may be achieved at a faster rate if our industries can serve a larger market and have access to a greater source of raw material resources. This is why we look to Indonesia, Malaya, Thailand, the Borneo territories and the rest of Southeast Asia for the future expansion of our industrial activities. Already we are selling to Indonesia our manufactured goods; already we are planning industrial projects to help develop Indonesia's fisheries, forest products, bauxite, etc.; already we are planning to displace Singapore as the trading center of Indonesia's entrepot trade. The Djakarta Agreement negotiated by the Hechanova Mission and the Manila Memorandum concluded with the Indonesian Economic and Trade Mission last year has opened the doors of unlimited opportunities for Filipino economic leadership in our part of the world.

Industrialization is sought to bring about a fuller and more prosperous life for our people; but under the free enterprise system, it gives the nation extra dividends. For industrialization brings about and is brought about in turn by the emergence of an entrepreneurial and managerial class — a financially independent and therefore intellectually independent middle class that strides the gap between the very rich and the very poor and guarantees the stability and permanence of our democratic way of life.

This, then, is our dream: A Philippines free from the shackles of a plantation economy, a modern industrialized nation recognized as a leader in Southeast Asia, and firmly committed to freedom, independence, nationalism and the democratic way of life.

THE WEALTH OF THE NATION

What constitutes the wealth of the nation?

Any foreign expert worth his commission will say of course that the wealth of the nation lies in its "natural resources" — in its mines, its forests, its fields and its waters.

He will say that there is a wealth of minerals still lying under our earth — ores of iron, nickel, manganese, copper, chrome, gold, coal, lime stones, asbestos — just waiting to be mined, shipped and bartered for all the stateside goodies that make life worthwhile for the Filipino.

He will say that there are still vast areas of age-old timber which stand waiting to be cut, fertile fields which with the help of imported fertilizers and insecticides will yield more sugar, more coconuts, more abaca and bananas for export, so that we can import more cars, more refrigerators and more TV sets.

If it is true that raw material resources constitute the wealth of the nation, then the Philippines and certainly its neighbor Indonesia, would be among the richest nations in the world today. Yet it is obvious that the Filipino and the Indonesian stand barefoot on the richest soil on earth.

Far richer are the Swiss, the Japanese and the British who have practically no natural resources to call their own.

With Fervor Burning

Switzerland is a land of picturesque snows and mountains, with no iron ore deposits. But the Swiss are rich, because they can buy 10 cents worth of steel from Sweden and make $10,000 worth of watch springs out of it. The difference between 10 cents and $10,000 is the extent of the wealth Swiss watchmakers derive from the skills they apply on that pound of steel.

The Japanese do not have iron ore deposits in their country either. But they buy iron from the Philippines at $10 per ton, and convert it into intricate steel machinery worth $3,000 per ton. And the difference between the $10 and $3,000 is the extent of the wealth the Japanese derive from the ton of ore for which the Filipinos were paid a measly $10.

The Japanese have neither the climate nor the land area needed to plant cotton. But they buy cotton from the United States, and manufacture textiles cheaper and better than those m the United States.

The British were once like the Filipinos — exporters of raw materials and importers of finished goods. In the 16th century, the British sent their iron ore to Germany to be made into metal ware, and their flax and wool to the Flemish weavers who converted them into cloth. But by deliberate statecraft, the British banned the export of iron ore, flax and wool, and embarked on the exploitation and development of their own labor skills. The iron and textile industries that came into being in Britain became the starting points for the birth of the First Industrial Revolution which made Great Britain the greatest nation of its time, mistress of all the seas and the lord of lands upon which the sun never set. The British Empire came about in the wake of a search for sources of raw materials and markets for British-made finished products.

What then constitutes the wealth of a nation?

The wealth of a nation does not so much consist of its raw material resources. *The wealth of a nation lies in the skills, the energy and the character of its people.*

With Fervor Burning

When we sell our iron ore to the Japanese, we are in effect selling them something that we have irretrievably lost. The more iron ore we mine and export, the less iron ore we have left for the use of future generations.

When the Japanese convert this iron ore to steel machinery and sell it back to us, they are in effect selling us the product of their skills, which is really never lost to them. For skills are a resource that grows by what it feeds on. The more skills the Japanese use, the more skilled they become. Skills are self-accumulating and self-perpetuating, and may be passed on from one generation to another, undiminished and everaugmented.

Thus countries like Japan which export their skills are getting richer and richer; while countries like the Philippines which export their natural resources, are getting poorer and poorer. So-called economists who glory in our favorable trade balance with Japan are fools not to mind this basic fact: What we sell to Japan (our materials) are irretrievably lost to us, what the Japanese sell to us (their skills) are never really lost to them.

Another basic difference between the wealth of raw material resources and the wealth of skills lies in their relationship to time and space.

A raw material is bounded by length, width and depth — the three dimensions of space. It can be seen, felt, weighed and most important, it can be stored. Our iron ore and other minerals, if not used today, are available for use in the future.

Our materials may lie under the earth awaiting the day we can economically develop them, but the labor value of an idle day is lost forever. For the wealth derived from skills is a function of the fourth dimension — time, ever elusive and ever fleeting.

Time lost is never regained. The wealth that might have been created by the skills of a man who is unemployed is irretrievably lost, unless a time machine is invented to turn the clock back.

In the Philippines, there are 600,000 laborers totally unemployed; 1,200,000 visibly underemployed, assumed to be at work only 50% of the time; and 5,600,000 farmers and members of their families helping in fanning operations who work only 4 months out of the year. Assuming that each is entitled to work 300 days a year, and capable at the level of their skills of creating wealth equivalent to P4 a day, the economic loss to our nation for the non-utilization of skills reaches a staggering P6 billion a year, about four times the entire revenue of our government, twice our entire export income and enough to increase our national income by almost 40%.

What are the lessons to be derived from all these?

1. That the policy of "developing our natural resources" should be subordinated to the policy of alleviating unemployment, even if this means using imported materials;

2. That, everything being equal, labor intensive industries are preferable to capital intensive industries;

3. That the much maligned "assembly" plants and beauty parlor industries are preferable to outright importation of finished goods, and are a necessary training ground for the development of entrepreneurial and labor skills;

4. And that foreign experts who want us to remain a raw-material exporting country under the guise of free trade, free enterprise, rural development, development of natural resources, the law of comparative advantage, priority of export industries and all such well-worn, self-serving cliches, are not serving the long-run interests of our country.

COMPARATIVE ADVANTAGE LAW

A free-for-all-light is of greatest advantage to one who is the biggest bully in the block.

In the same manner, Free Trade is of greatest advantage to an industrial colossus among backward nations.

Thus, during the era of Pax Britannia, when Great Britain was the greatest industrial nation on the face of the earth, the British never tired of lecturing the rest of the world about the folly of protecting infant industries and the advantages of free trade. To bolster their thesis, the British promulgated the so-called "Law of Comparative Advantage" to prove that free trade is the most natural and scientific method of conducting international economic relations.

The great German economist, Friedrich List, borrowing some of his ideas from two distinguished American economists, Alexander Hamilton and Mathew Carey, protested at the time that "The Law of Comparative Advantage was a British doctrine, designed to prevent the growth of other industrial nations that might destroy Great Britain's world monopoly of manufacturing."

It is interesting to note that the United States and Germany did not heed British advice and as a matter of fact did embark on a policy of protectionism during the latter half of the nineteenth century to emerge as part of that concert of countries known as the industrialized nations of the West.

It is even more interesting to note that today, citizens of industrialized nations are in turn lecturing us poor Filipinos about the folly of protecting our local industries and the advantage of free trade and unfettered free enterprise. And to advance this thesis, cocktail cowboys and after-dinner party philosophers employed by foreign firms are sanctimoniously spreading the gospel of the "Law of Comparative

Advantage," as if it were the Ten Commandments.

What is the Law of Comparative Advantage?

Stated simply, the Law of Comparative Advantage is this: Every nation should concentrate on producing goods that it can by experience produce most cheaply, exporting its surplus of such goods in exchange for other goods which it can produce only at a greater cost.

Thus, the Law states, there would be "maximum international division of labor" with each nation producing the greatest output for the least effort, resulting in the highest possible level of total world production and consumption.

This Law is offered as a universal rule, applicable to all times, all places and all conditions — and therein lies its fallacy.

In the first place, the Law presumes that there exists in all countries "full employment of labor and material resources," so that a country which starts a new industry would have to divert resources from other industries in which such resources are already fully and efficiently employed.

But such is not the case as far as the Philippines and other underdeveloped countries are concerned. The Philippines has a reserve of unemployed and underemployed labor which consume but does not produce, and will not otherwise be utilized to good purpose unless channeled into new industries. At the same time, we have a wealth of raw material resources which have largely been untapped because we have no industries to make use of them, nor has it served the interest of other countries to import them from us.

Secondly, the Law presumes that every country is of the same stage of technological development from which to compete with equal opportunity for success.

Free trade between an industrial colossus and a backward nation is analogous to pitting an ignorant child against a well-educated adult It simply is not fair. The child must be supported through school until he gets an education that will enable him to compete with a fair chance of success.

An entrepreneur in the Philippines, setting up a new industry is likely to be a self-made manager with little practical experience in the industry he is establishing. He recruits his labor force from the province where people know little of machinery and have no experience with the rigid discipline of the factory.

It may take a generation before he can really have a level of managerial competence and a skilled and discipline labor force comparable to those in the United States.

More often than not, his factory site lacks good roads, water, power, telephone facilities; he often has to develop his own sources of materials and establish his own marketing facilities — all the "external economies" that are taken for granted and available cheaply in industrialized countries. He is likely to find that the necessary capital and credit are difficult and expensive to obtain, because of the lack of institutions that can mobilize savings — if indeed enough savings can be mobilized in a country when most of the people live from hand to mouth.

These factors and many more — including a colonial mentality that saps his self-confidence — constitute a serious handicap that must be made up by some measure of protectionism until the Filipino entrepreneur can compete effectively in the markets of the world.

Free trade such as existed between the United States and the Philippines during the 50 years of American occupation has made the Philippines an exporter of raw materials and an importer of finished goods, even our basic necessities. There are many disadvantages to this:

1. As we pointed out in a previous essay, we are

poorer by the exchange of our depletable raw materials for the products of American skills (a resource that is self-perpetuating);

2. The prices of raw materials fluctuate unpredictably in the world markets while those of manufactured goods are relatively steady, thus giving an element of instability that can easily lead to the deterioration of the state of our economy;

3. Wars, depressions, shipping cartels and economic blackmail by industrialized countries constantly threaten to cut off the markets for our raw materials and sources of the essential commodities which we have to import in order to survive;

4. Worst of all, it leaves us helpless before the rank hypocrisy of those who would, for all those 50 years, decree free trade for all the products they export to us while imposing quotas on our major exports such as sugar — those who would demand equal rights with us citizens of a backward country while enjoying a competitive advantage over the Japanese and others who are their technological equals and natural competitors — those who would protect their own agricultural produce with scandalous subsidies and protest vigorously when we do the same for our tobacco — and who would then have the God-awful cheek to assault our intelligence with sanctimonious and pompous preachments about the Law of Comparative Advantage and Free Trade which they never really do practice.

THE TARIFF AS PROTECTOR

The climax occurred at 2:30 A.M., July 9, 1964, when Speaker Cornelio Villareal banged the gavel angrily, ordered the doors of the session hall closed and sent out the sergeant-at-arms to arrest enough congressmen to constitute a quorum. By 6 A.M., sleepy-eyed congressmen filed out of the Chamber, content with the realization that for the first time since 1957, for the second time since 1909, and after three almost fruitless years of deliberation, the Omnibus Tariff Bill was finally passed by the legislature.

The anti-climax came at midnight on Saturday, Aug. 8, 30 days after the adjournment of the second special session, when President Macapagal, after receiving the enrolled copy of the bill barely one and a half hours before deadline, complained of lack of time to study its implications, and mindful of rumors of "smuggled" insertions, was constrained to veto the measure. President Macapagal, however, ordered the National Economic Council to prepare an Executive Order for the readjustment of tariff duties along the lines suggested by the Omnibus Tariff Bill.

Yet behind all these is still a strong undercurrent of feeling among some opinion-makers that somehow, tariff protection prejudices the interest of the consumer in favor of "greedy" local producers. As a matter of fact there is a tendency at times to regard the whole program of industrialization and economic protectionism as a conspiracy against the consumer.

Why should this be so? We are all consumers, every single blessed one of us 30 million Filipinos. But among us consumers, there are those who do not produce. And it is properly the economic policy of the government to encourage non-producers to produce, and producers to produce more.

An industrial pioneer, as we mentioned before, by the very act of pioneering is initially the first and only manufacturer in the field. But he is not a monopolist, for nobody is prevented to come and compete with him. And certainly, with high enough tariff walls, the government may encourage the entry of more competitors in the industrial field. The other alternative would be to allow local producers to succumb to unfair foreign competition.

By all means, let us have free competition among Filipino producers employing Filipino laborers, with all the confidence that such competition will eventually lower prices to the consumer. For raising our standard of living does not only mean lower prices on the goods we buy, but also increased wages from the job opportunities we create. And someday we shall realize that a nation of consumers who are not also producers is a nation of parasites.

In these days of decontrol, the most important incentive to local production is an adequate tariff protection. The United States, at its formative period of development from the close of the Civil War up to the end of the 19th century, imposed high tariff walls to encourage local production. According to the Encyclopedia Britannica, Vol. 22, page 808, we quote the following passage: "The duties on imports were driven higher than the original Merrill Tariff had ever contemplated. The average rates . . . rose ... to nearly 50 per cent on dutiable articles and 35 per cent on the aggregate. Domestic manufacturers sprang into new life under such encouragement; everyone who had spare wealth converted it to manufacturing capital . . ." The McKinley Tariff of 1890, the Wilson Tariff of 1893 and the Dingley Tariff Act of 1897 "raised duties to their highest point," till at last by 1900, as the Britannica says on page 825 of the same volume, "economic prosperity and far reaching processes of social change" made the United States turn to "consider its position as a world power."

In its formative period of development, the United States imposed a weighted average rate of 35 per cent on all aggregate imports, that is to say, total duties collected amounted to 35 per cent of total value of imports.

What is our average rate of duty in the

Philippines?

During the period from 1958 to 1963 inclusive, the Philippines imported goods worth P8,522,811,588 in FOB value, and collected customs duties amounting to PI,028,832,400. The average rate of duty during this period is 12 per cent on value of goods imported.

While the United States in a comparable period of development imposed tariff duties at the average rate of 35 per cent, we in the Philippines imposed only 12 per cent. When we consider that most of our imports we undervalued when declared, and earlier priced at an artificial rate of P2 to $1, then our average tariff rate on value of imports must have been lower than statistics would show.

If the Filipino industrialist is to grow strong enough to meet world competition, he must have a home to grow in and to call his own, his own castle to defend, a fortress from which to sally forth into the arena of world trade.

The home market is his castle, and there must he reign supreme or perish with our people in the dungeons of economic bondage.

German and Japanese cameras compete in Hongkong but not in Germany or Japan.

English and American cars compete in Europe but not in England or America.

The contending armies of economic competition meet in fields of battle other than their own respective home grounds.

Our home market, our castle, must have walls of tariff protection high enough to discourage competitive imported goods and encourage investments in local production.

Thus we await with eager anticipation, another Tariff Proclamation, another Executive Order adjusting tariff rates on the ever growing list of local manufactures, with the assurance that behind those tariff walls many skills will be given opportunity to flourish and in the great diversity of goods that we produce for our home market, we shall find the products that we can produce cheaper and better than the rest of the world.

ARE FILIPINOS REALLY POOR?

How poor is the Philippines? How rich is the United States? For the poor Filipino, mesmerized by Hollywood and Madison Avenue, the questions might as well be: how deep is the ocean and how high is the sky?

The American looks up his statistical tables, slides his rule, totes up his figures in regimented columns, and comes up with the incontrovertible answers:

The Philippines has a per capita income of only $120 per annum, the United States has an enormous $2413 income per capita. Each American commands the use of good and services 20 times as much as each poor Filipino. With six times the population of the Philippines, the United States has a national income of 120 times that of the Philippines. The statistics are enough to make every Filipino wallow in envy, self-pity and mendacity.

National income statistics are often used by economists in evaluating the comparative wealth and economic well-being of countries and peoples. But the standard methods of national income accounting usually and necessarily differentiate between goods and services bought and sold in the market, and identical goods and services that do not enter the market at all. The value of the former appears in the compilation of statistics; the latter does not.

In other words the national income rises when a man eats in a restaurant; and the national income falls when he cooks his own food.

Thus, in a non-industrial country like the Philippines where most people with the help of their neighbors build their own houses, plant and harvest their own crops without money ever changing hands, there is a tremendous amount of unbought goods and services that never gets registered in national income statistics.

Furthermore, in a highly monetized and sophisticated economy like the United States, goods undergo long and complicated processes all paid with money before they reach the final consumer.

Let's take a simple case, the consumption of an egg. The egg on the breakfast table of the ordinary American has been washed, graded, inspected, trucked, refrigerated, stored, packed, displayed and sold through various channels. The egg on the breakfast table of the ordinary Filipino probably dropped straight from the chicken to the skillet.

Take another example, the consumption of pork. The American pig is fed with commercial feed, pampered by paid veterinarians and experts in animal husbandry, is sold to a meatpacking plant where it is slaughtered, cut ground, cooked and packed in tin cans which in turn are stored and sold through a chain of jobbers, wholesalers and retailers before it is eaten by the American consumer.

In the Philippines, the pig is kept under the house unattended, fed with left-over food, slaughtered in the backyard and cooked by its owner before it is eaten and offered free to relatives and neighbors. No cash passes hands, no increase in national income is ever registered.

The money values added to the egg and the pig as consumer in the United States are considerably more than in the Philippines and therefore contribute to a greater extent to the national income of the United States, even though the satisfaction and well-being derived from the consumption of such commodities are the same in the United States and the Philippines.

Multiply this situation with the hundreds of thousands of other commodities needed for life and limb, and it is easy to realize how differences in economic sophistication can result in great disparity of national income.

Also, tertiary industries in the United States are increasing their relative share of the total national income. Relatively more Americans than Filipinos eat in restaurant rather than cook their own food; send their clothes to the laundry instead of washing them at home; bum high octane gasoline instead of walking or cycling; buy phonograph records instead of serenading each other; go to the movies and theaters to buy the services of paid performers instead of singing, dancing, playing or gossiping for each other's entertainment; go to hotels and motels instead of open fields and relatives' houses; buy books or watch television instead of listening to village idiots, philosophers and politicians. All of which enter the money economy and are duly entered in the accounting records of the national income, much more in the United States than in the Philippines.

Lastly, to paraphrase the words of Professor William Letwin of MIT, the warm and wonderful climate of the Philippines places in the hands of the Filipino, almost without asking, a plentiful supply of plants and animals, not only in one short season, but throughout the year. His needs for food, clothing and shelter are relatively simple and readily supplied.

It is a colossal exercise in irony, says Letwin, that the people of the United States, having deliberately planted themselves in a comparatively inhospitable region, are now forced to overcome the hazards of their environment by wearing thick woolen underwear, coats, overcoats, mittens and overshoes — by erecting beehives of concrete with central heating and a maze of plumbing — by forcing crops out of a reluctant earth through use of fertilizers, tractors and enormous combines — by lending a little cheer to their lives with jets, pets, hi-fi sets, sherbets, corsets, hairnets, horse bets and bulls —.

And as Letwin puts it, having produced all these things, the need for which was imposed only by the unsuitable setting in which they perversely decided to live, they have weighed all these goods and finding them many (and duly registered tier upon tier in their national income statistics) — they now proclaim themselves rich and call upon us poor Filipinos to emulate them.

But why are we Filipinos in fact so poor?

The answer is that only in such countries as the Philippines can a people be so poor and still continue to live without despair, deriving strength from an aroused hope to pursue a better tomorrow.

OUR ECONOMY, BETTER THAN WE THOUGHT?

It is a matter of record that the rate of our economic growth in 1963 was 4.8 per cent But there is at least one person who thinks that our economic growth was much better than we thought, perhaps 10.9 per cent!

It is a matter of record that in the same year, our manufacturing output increased by 6.4 per cent. This same person feels it is closer to 16.7 per cent!

This person also believes that throughout the decade 1953 to 1963, the growth of our economy has been substantially greater than we generally supposed, particularly with respect to the manufacturing sector. He believes further that our record of impressive growth was probably the highest in Asia and Africa, and that the year 1963 was "the year of greatest growth that this country has ever experienced."

Who is he? Not Armand Fabella, not Feny Hechanova, not Andy Castillo, not yours truly, Larry Henares either, nor any spokesman of this Administration.

He is James Warren, Jr., an economist who is connected with the ESSO beehive on United Nations Avenue. He is one American we know who neither boasts nor bluffs, and is remarkably devoid of prejudice, arrogance or condescension. His paper on "Energy and Economic Advance" is recommended reading for open-minded Filipino economists.

Measuring economic growth is a tricky business. The accepted and conventional method is to measure the increase in the "gross national product" (GNP) which is the totality of the volume (or value at constant prices) of all goods and services produced in the country for a given year. Obviously, it is impossible to account for every single product made and every service rendered in the country during the whole year. So instead of counting them all, the authorities resort to "statistical sampling," e.g, assume that a few randomly selected firms represent a whole industrial field. Errors are bound to creep in, although this is supposedly minimized by scientific selection of the samples taken.

Now, Mr. Warren advances the thesis that the consumption of energy, such as hydro-electricity, coal and petroleum fuels, is somehow proportioned to the level of goods and services produced in the Philippines.

Wlty not? Fuel oil, coal and electricity provide power for the manufacturing sector. Diesel oil and electricity go into the mining sector; kerosene, a home-cooking fuel, into the household consumption sector; automotive diesel oil and gasoline, into the transportation and agricultural sectors; thermal and hydro-electric power into household consumption, industry and commerce; industrial diesel oil and fuel oil into railroads and coastal shipping.

But what is most intriguing is that statistics on energy consumption are "hard" statistics, that is, available almost in its entirety rather than the representative sampling. All we have to do is to get the information from a relatively few oil companies, the National Power Corporation and the Meralco — and presto, we have the figures on almost all the total energy consumed in the Philippines.

Warren took all such statistics for the period 1953 to 1963, converted them all into common "fuel oil equivalent" units, computed the yearly increase of energy consumption during the period, and compared the latter with the yearly increase in GNP, with these results:

YEAR	% INCREASE IN ENERGY CONSUMPTION	% INCREASE GNP
1954	7.0%	5.4%
1955	9.1%	7.8%
1956	9.5%	5.1%
1957	10.7%	4.4%
1958	8.5%	4.2%
1959	7.7%	5.9%
1960	6.6%	2.8%
1961	6.9%	5.8%
1962	8.6%	4.4%
1963	10.9%	4.8%

The compound growth rate for consumption of commercial energy in the Philippines for the indicated period was 8.8% per year. By comparison, for the period 1950 to I960, the comparative growth rates for other countries were as follows: Japan, 12% per year; India, 5.9%; Malaya, 5.9%; Australia, 5.2%. For the whole East and South Africa, the South and Southeast Asia, Oceania and Japan, the aggregate growth rate was only 6.5% per year.

Clearly, the Philippine performance is absolutely phenomenal.

Turning to a sub-sector of the economy, the manufacturing sector, the record is even more impressive. The following table shows the yearly increase of energy consumed by the manufacturing industries, as compared with increases in the official Central Bank indices on physical volume of manufacturers:

YEAR	% INCREASE IN INDUSTRIAL ENERGY	% INCREASE IN OFFICIAL INDEX OF MANUFACTURING
1954	12.1%	12.4%
1955	95%	12.6%
1956	12.2%	15.7%
1957	26.4%	8.0%
1958	21.1%	7.7%
1959	15.7%	83%
1960	10.2%	33%
1961	14.7%	6.6%
1962	11.2%	5.7%
1963	16.7%	6.4%

Warren feels that there should have been very much closer correlation between measurable inputs of commercial energy and the official figures of the government on GNP and index of manufacturing.

He is particularly disturbed at the divergence of his figures and those of the government in the manufacturing sector. Particularly since the government figures indicate a "slow down," while his figures on consumption indicate a "real boom" economy. He asks: What did the industries do with all those demonstrably larger volumes of energy input in each of the recent years?

Electricity cannot be stockpiled. Coal has limited possibilities of being stockpiled. And oil storage facilities are prohibitively expensive to stockpile.

No, the electricity was used. The coal and oil were burned. And the energy generated moved machines, activated motors, gave heat, turned wheels — and produced goods and goods and more goods.

And it would seem, in spite of official statistics and all the breast-beating about the "slow down of activity after decontrol," that the Philippine economic growth has been phenomenally strong even up to the present time.

Warren's thesis, of course, has its qualification. There is, for example, the possible substitution between statistically recorded energy (such as kerosene) and non-statistically recorded energy (such as home-made charcoal or firewood). There is the possibility that there are new energy-intensive industries (such as calcium carbide or synthetic fertilizer plants, of which there are very few) which change the proportion between energy consumed and amount of goods produced. And of course, there is the difficulty of ascertaining whether the gasoline bought by a factory was used to transport products to the customer or to bring the factory owner to the Kahirup Ball.

By and large, Warren believes, his possible "errors" are small compared to those of government statistics. And it is his judgment that the official figures do not do justice to the economy's true growth, not only in the overall picture, but especially in industry and manufacturing.

Looking at all the thousands of humming factories from as far north as Bacnotan to as far south as Davao, the fantastic diversity of the goods they produce and the job opportunities they opened to the people — and realizing how much better fed, better clothed, better housed are the Filipinos compared to a decade ago — we are tempted to agree with Mr. Warren.

But why then all the gripes, breast-beating, and sleepless nights spent on tight credit, smuggling decontrol and cut-throat competition? Are these signs of prosperity and growth?

Perhaps, our nation is still in the teen-age time of its life. Remember that awkward age when we as teenagers spent sleepless nights worrying about body odor, bad breath, unrequited love and pimples that assumed the proportions of May on Volcano?

We did not realize it then, and our nation does not realize it now — but teen-age time, in spite of its dreadful anxieties, is the time of greatest growth and miraculous flowering.

A THOUSAND TOMORROWS

The art of politics, according to John Emmet Hughes, *is not to mend the petty conflicts of the moment, nor to close some tiny gap in the discourse of the day — but to define and to advance designs and policies for a thousand tomorrows.*

Unfortunately, postwar politics in the Philippines had been full of the sound and fury of petty conflicts and daily discourse, and not much else. No great leader ever stayed in power long enough to marshal the energies and resources of the people behind a national purpose designed for a "thousand tomorrows."

The two popular presidents (before Diosdado Mrcapagal) who were carried to the crest of national leadership on a wave of mass enthusiasm, died tragically before the end of their first term of office. The two vice presidents who followed in their wake, were tried, found wanting and rejected by the people before they reached the constitutional limits of a second term in office.

As a result, the Philippines — the first colony to achieve postwar independence, the most literate and the best financed at the outset of its nationhood — floundered in a morass of cross-purposes and failed to achieve the kind of progress attained by Nehru's India, Nasser's Egypt, Ben Gurion's Israel, Adenaur's Germany, de Gaulle's France or even Chiang's Taiwan.

It was not always thus in the Philippines.

In 1916, a young man named Manuel L. Quezon, after showing his mettle as resident commissioner to the United States, was unanimously elected as president of the Senate, the highest post held by a Filipino at the time. For the next 28 years, he provided a firm leadership for a mass movement that led to this nation's political independence.

It seems rather surprising to us now how his followers managed to keep him at the helm — first as Senate president for 18 years, then as Commonwealth President for a term of six years, then with a change in the Constitution for another term as four years, then by an extension of his term in wartime Washington to the end of his days. He ruled practically through a one-party government by the consent of his people, and never once was seriously regarded as a dictator. He was, like Roosevelt and most great leaders of his stature, President unto death.

But what was his legacy to this nation? A reason for being a justification of its existence as a nation, a national purpose. It was Quezon who unified his people, set up the political institutions of self government, and set the stage for our national political independence.

What of the present?

The postwar lack of sustained leadership has

left our nation rudderless in its pursuit of economic independence and national dignity — our people ambivalent with a schizophrenic split-personality, torn between the wide open challenge of true sovereignty and the claustrophobic security of a mother's womb — our economic efforts stunted between the pastoral peace of a feudal economy and the demanding disciplines of an industrial society — our democratic way of life threatened on one hand by communist subversion, and bulldozed on the other by McCarthyists through fear, smear and economic black-mail.

We have fallen into the rut of thinking politically in terms of tight compartments of four years' duration, charging our elective officials with full accounting of everything that happens within their term of office. We do not seem to realize that the solutions to the problems that plague our society have a longer gestation period — that the ills we suffer now may be the legacy of a previous administration, and that the benefits of the good we do today may only be reaped by some future administration. Thus overly concerned with the weeds of today, we fail to plant the seeds for tomorrow's harvest.

Today is all we have, so we grab all we can and hold on with shameless despair. We are adrift in an ocean of nothingness and we hang on to any miserable piece of wreckage as if it were the tree of life. We who are without hope are driven to desperate self-seeking like the enslaved Hebrews in Egypt, "their lives made bitter with hard bondage."

We need a Moses to unite us in common hope for a promised land and to set our eyes, not on today's ignominy, but on a glorious vision of a thousand tomorrows.

Is President Diosdado Macapagal such a leader?

Macapagal was a vice president who did not

succeed to the Presidency by the death of his predecessor, as did Elpidio Quirino and Carlos P. Garcia.

He came to power, more like Manuel Roxas and Ramon Magsaysay, by the overwhelming verdict of the electorate and buoyed up on the hopes of his people.

But unlike Roxas and Magsaysay, he is living out his first term of office and has already earned a place in history as the first postwar President to chart an independent course in foreign policy, achieving a measure of leadership in Southeast Asia; to break the 400-year old feudal structure of our society through the passage of the Land Reform Code; to promulgate the first officially adopted socio-economic program for an all-out industrialization.

Macapagal now seeks his second and last term of office. If he wins, he will be the first postwar President of the Republic to extend his leadership to the constitutional limits of a second term — and will serve four years without the political imperatives that plague one who seeks re-election, and may give this nation a sustained leadership which we hope will be carried on by his successors with constancy and consistency of purpose.

A thousand tomorrows hence, may it not be said that our politicians squandered their energies in petty conflicts and daily discourse, and failed at the most crucial time in our history to set the stage for the fulfillment of our people's aspirations — that in the blindness of their intramural squabbles, they have shattered the course of industrialization, dimmed the cause of nationalism and doomed to abortion the birth of the nation. May it rather be said, that our politicians, regardless of party or personality, under the inspired leadership of our duly elected leaders, did unite in common cause for the common good, that our nation may survive and prosper for a thousand tomorrows till the end of time.   -----

Hilarion (Larry) M. Henares Jr.   83

PARKINSON'S INTERESTING LAW

Students of the contemporary scene are often amazed at the ungovernable tendency of government entities and personnel to proliferate like rabbits and tilapia on a diet of durian.

In 1930, the government had 29,419 employees and an annual budget of P78 million; in 1960, it had 361,312 employees and a budget of Pl,333 million. During the 30-year period in which population increased by a mere 109 per cent, the number of government employees increased by 1,128 per cent and the annual budget by 1,353 per cent.

This is a phenomenon we witness not only in the Philippines but also in other countries of the world. And it leads the taxpayer to conclude either (hopefully) that the average citizen is enjoying vastly greater government services than ever before, or (rather cynically) that government employees are working fewer hours and devoting more time to loafing and mischief.

Whatever his conclusions may be, the taxpayer's reasoning is not valid according to Prof. C. Northcote Parkinson, economist, management expert, and philosopher of delightful wit and mock-solemn wisdom.

For it is the contention of Parkinson that the proliferation of government entities and personnel follow an immutable law that has absolutely nothing to do with the amount of services actually rendered; and that Big Brother Government, like Topsy, will inexorably grow by fantastic proportions whether the volume of work to be done increases, decreases, or disappears altogether.

Parkinson's Law on pyramidal organization growth is based on two observable and demonstrable facts of official human behavior:

1. An official wants to multiply subordinates, not rivals.

With Fervor Burning

2. Officials make work for each other.

To illustrate the way Parkinson's Law operates, let us narrate what happens to a typical government official, Mr. A, who feels he is being abused and overworked.

He could ask for a raise in pay, of course, but he will not get it.

He could resign, but he won't.

He could ask for the appointment of a colleague to help him in his work, but why should he? That would bring in someone who is a potential rival when the time comes to ask for a promotion.

So what does he do? He demands the appointment of at least two subordinates to do his job for him. Why two? One subordinate may prove to be damnably indispensable and possibly pose a threat to his own position. But two subordinates may be kept in check by playing on the jealousy of one against the other.

So Mr. A, arranges to have two subordinates under him — Mr. B and Mr. C.

Now, Mr. B will in the course of time feel abused and overworked and he in turndemands and gets two subordinates of his own — Mr. D and Mr. E.

Mr. C of course will get jealous, and whether he needs them or not, he will also demand and get two subordinates of his own — Mr. F andMr. G.

Thus seven officialsare now doing what one used to do before. Will the work be done faster and easier? Of course not. For these seven men make so much work for each other than every one   of them is fully occupied, and Mr. A finds that he is working harder than he ever did when he had to do the work alone by himself.

Mr. D receives a document and decides after laborious thinking, that it does not lie within his competence to answer, so he passes it on to Mr. E who makes a draft of a reply and hands it to Mr. B, who

With Fervor Burning

initials it and passes it on to Mr. A. Mr. A wants it checked by Mr. C who hands it to Mr. F for checking and to Mr. G for redrafting. Mr. G now sends the papers back to Mr. C who initials the draft and lays the papers on the desk of Mr. A.

And what does Mr. A do? He reads the draft, crosses out the inconsequentials and irrelevances, corrects the English, rearranges the paragraphs, reads it again and disgustedly throws it in the wastebasket Thereupon he wrinkles his eyebrow, sharpens his pencil and proceeds to write out the same reply he might have written if Messrs. B, C, D, E, F, G had never been born.

But Mr. A has extra problems on his mind. He now has to contend with the office intrigues of Mr. B, the absenteeism of Mr. C, the philanderings of Mr. D, the unauthorized use of the telephone by Mr. E, the petty thievery of Mr. F, and the bad breath and body odor of Mr. G.

Thus more people consume longer time to produce the same result No one has been idle and all have done their best. Mr. A is far more overworked than he was at the beginning. But he is happy, for now he is the manager of a department with six men under him. And he can now, with more reason, demand and get a raise in pay which he would have never deserved if he was content to do the job all by his lonesome self.

Thus is stated Parkinson's Law: "Work expands so as to fill the time available for its completion."

One does not have to poke around government offices to get proof of this. One only has to observe the difference between a busy businessman and his socialite wife.

The businessman who has little time to spare, can write a postcard in three minutes flat.

His socialite wife who has all the time m the world may spend an hour looking for the postcard, another hour looking for a ball pen and her eyeglasses, two hours lying in bed wondering what to write about, another two hours actually writing the message, one hour looking for the address of the person she wants to mail it to, another hour looking for a stamp, and the rest of her waking hours making up her mind whether to mail it or not. And she ends the day in a state of absolute exhaustion.

Thus Parkinson follows up with interesting corollaries to his law:

1. "There need be little or no relationship between the work to be done and the size of the staff to which it is assigned."

2. "A lack of real activity does not, of necessity, result in leisure."

3. "A lack of occupation is not necessarily revealed by a manifest idleness."

4. "The thing to be done swells in importance and complexity in direct ratio with the time to be spent in doing it"

FROM ONE MAN TO TEAM WORK

Every business firm starts its growth under the highly personalized leadership of one man. Inevitably, however, the time comes when the personal leader gives way to an "organization man and his management team."

This shift from the leadership of one personality to that of a management team comes as part of the natural process of growth, but is rarely as smooth as some people think. It is often a painful and laborious process that starts with the refusal of the personal leader to abdicate his power and position, a breakdown of the organization sometimes to the verge of bankruptcy, a vacuum of leadership and a struggle for power, quite analogous to the bloody revolutions that new nations of Asia and Africa have experienced within our lifetime.

There are many classic examples of how personal leadership gives way to the organization man and his management team.

General Henry Du Pont who started a chemical complex bearing his name, was a man of fabulous capacity. He personally directed a highly centralized organization where decisions were made at the top, and subordinates are judged, not by some impersonal and pre-formulated criteria, but by how "I (the personal leader) who would have done it if I had the time to do it myself." General Du Pont reviewed all chemical formulations (300 every day); he interviewed, hired and fired all personnel; wrote every letter in longhand and bought the stamps himself; and approved every expenditure down to 10 cents. He was still doing it when he died. His son, Eugene Du Pont, tried to run the company the same way, and it killed him. He just didn't have the capacity of his father and he died shortly of ulcers. And the Du Pont Co. went into bankruptcy. Three Du Pont cousins bought out the assets and brought the company through the period of transition to a "management-team leadership."

Another example is that of the automobile industry in the United States. In 1923. General Motors, an unwieldy combine of car factories, was under the personal leadership of Walter C. Durant, a master salesman who sold more cars than any man in history. He also sold the company almost into bankruptcy and General Motors was, for the second time, at the verge of extinction. Then Alfred B. Sloan, an organization man, carried the company through the transition to management team leadership.

Ford Motor Co., the oldest car manufacturer in the world, grew to become a giant under the personal leadership of Henry Ford I, a mechanical genius who had his own ideas about car styles and labor relations.

With Fervor Burning

It is a tribute to the capacity of this man that his company survived up to 1946 when he died. By that time the Ford Company was losing $9 million a month and sinking fast, until Henry Ford II carried it through the crisis and made an amazing comeback under a management team.

Other firms went through their crises and never recovered. Out of 2,942 car companies that existed since 1899, only five exist today in the United States. And these five exist today by virtue of their ability to make this judgement towards management team leadership.

Students of the management movement in the Philippines may well look into the cases of the many big firms here that experienced or are about to experience this crisis of management transition — the rubber shoe manufacturer who branched out into steel and chemicals; the brewery magnate who still exercises effective personal leadership over a fabulous industrial empire; a brotherhood that started in the undertaker and refrigerator business and wound up with a complex of marketing, finance and industrial firms.

All these firms — Du Pont, General Motors, Ford — found out the hard way that management is a profession in itself and that a manager does not necessarily have to be an engineer, an accountant or a marketing man; that a company cannot progress on the opportunities of the moment and that advances in business must be planned and provided for in the future by acts that are done today; that management control should be in the terms, not of personal judgment, but of the dollar and cents of profit realization; and finally, that there must be an organizational provision for the inevitable transition from the personal leadership of one man to the leadership of an organization man and his team.

THE FUNCTIONAL ORGANIZATION

It is a fact that most organizations just happen. An organization just grows around people; then new people change it. No two organizations are alike, any more than two houses are alike; but a sound structure and foundation adapt to all kinds of houses and all kinds of organizations. Organizations are of many classifications — line and staff, committee, centralized or decentralized, vertical or horizontal.

But a brilliant young management authority named Louis A. Allen put forth the thesis that all such organizations are either one of two types; that we have really no choice between these two types of organizations, because we must adopt them both; management authority that we must start with one, and then at some time in the life of the organization, adopt the other; and that the transition between the two is a time of crisis where failure may mean bankruptcy, and where we must, if we are to survive, bridge the transition from personal leadership to the leadership of a management team.

The first of these two types is the "functional" type of organizational structure, where organizational groupings are made on the basis of the kinds of work to be performed. A manager of a small firm who does his own production supervision, his own accounting and his own selling, finds later that he no longer has the physical time nor the capacity to cope with the work; he then hires specialists — a production manager, an accountant and a sales manager. What the manager does at this stage is not to hire professional managers, but professional specialists, mere extensions of his power and function at a highly personal leader of the organization.

The functional type of organizational structure is ideal at this stage when the company is still in its formative period under a highly personalized leadership.

With Fervor Burning

It is the most direct, the fastest acting, the least demanding and the fastest growing of organizational structures. It simplifies training by encouraging specialization and places specialists in top management positions. It maximizes the span of command, and minimizes levels of management — if it can — for the spiraling and pyramiding can sometimes add up, as it did in the case of General Motors, to 19 levels of organization between the Board of Directors down to the worker at the operative level.

Because this functional structure is built like a pyramid, decisions, even minor decisions, tend to be forced up to the apex. This is fun as long as high personal leadership exists. As soon as it outgrows the scope of such individual, the organization breaks down.

This is where the transition starts, not before. When the firm grows in size and diversity of activities develop to a point beyond the capacity of one man to control, the functional structure begins to show its defects. For one thing, there are a few positions where decisions are made and specialists are not necessarily good managers. This type of organization, built around specialists, does not encourage the development of professional managers.

For another, how can you measure the performance of each functional unit in terms of pesos and centavos? The Accounting, the Production Department, the Sales Department — all depend and interact on each other for the realization of profits. The organization becomes harder to control.

And most of all, an overgrown functional organization with its pyramid of innumerable levels of management, inevitably suffers from line loss. The line of communication from the apex of the pyramid to the operative base becomes longer and weaker. Facts and the decisions based on facts, traveling through this long line of communication, become distorted and outdated, plagued with loss of meaning and loss of time. The pyramid which was its strength, becomes eventually the weakness of the functional type of organizational structure.

MANAGEMENT TEAM EMERGES

We expounded last week on the thesis that a business organization grows to a point when the functional organization under a highly personal leadership of one man finally breaks down and the time comes for a change in its organizational structure paving the way for the leadership of a management team.

The symptoms that call for the change are:

1. More and more decisions are forced to the top; the manager complains of overwork, and frustration over misunderstood instructions and delay in communications; this in turn is followed by

2. The appointment of assistants, an army of assistants doing the same thing and acting in the name of the manager;

3. The proliferation of committees, coordinators and liaison men to effect coordination between levels of management, bypassing the line of authority and responsibility.

When these symptoms appear, the time has come for a change, or the company plunges headlong into a crisis.

The time finally comes to reorganize and adopt the second type of organizational structure — the "divisionalized" type of organization, where organizational groupings are made on the basis of product groups or on the basis of geographic location, each a complete unit catering to a special need. General Electric has 193 product groupings; General Motors has a division for each make of car, each division having its own sales, production, financing and complete unto itself. Sears and Roebuck, and various banks and insurance companies, have branches that are physically apart from each other and autonomous in their operations.

The divisionalized structure in effect pushes decision-making down to the lower levels; authority and responsibility are placed closer to the actual operations; more capable and really professional managers are required, managers who may be shifted from one division to another with impunity. The Buick manager may take the place of the Chevrolet manager, but the production manager is not interchangeable with the sales manager.

The divisionalized structure of organization therefore is very much like an amoeba which divides itself into complete units, each with a new functional structure of its own and a renewed capacity for growth. But it no longer needs a highly personal leadership at the top, it now needs an "organization man" and a management team, totally divorced from the complications of specialized operating work, and concentrating on the main business of managing.

Thus, into full flower blossoms the true professional manager.

ECONOMISTS AND THEIR ROLE

A politician once remarked that an economist is like a eunuch, the manless man who guards the sultan's harem. The economist, he said, like the eunuch, knows what is going on, gossips about it, gives advice about how it is done, but he cannot do it himself.

I do not agree with the politician. Any observer of the public scene in recent years knows that it is the economist who provoked the public scene to begin with, and created a disturbance of the peace of mind of this generation of Filipinos. The great economic debates that raged in the public square between such economist as Cuademo, Araneta, Montelibano and others, did prod the country, almost against its will, to meet the challenge of change in the postwar years. No, these economists are no eunuchs, they are more like the eager and demanding wives of the sultan who nag him to fresh and greater efforts.

Whatever it is that economists are debating about, there seems to be one thing that they all agree on: That the Philippines must industrialize.

We must industrialize because unlike agriculture, every industry begets other industries as man begets children; because industry is the only economic activity that will keep pace with our population growth the rate of which is the highest in the world.

We must industrialize because we must diversify and expand our sources of income; because the primary exports from which we earn our living, are subject to wide fluctuations of price and volume in the world markets beyond our control, and can no longer be depended upon to provide a rising level of income for our people.

We must industrialize because it is the only way out of the plantation type of feudal economy, imposed upon us through centuries of colonial dependence during which we suffered untold poverty, ignorance and injustice.

We must industrialize because we need an industrial middleclass, a financially and intellectually independent middleclass to stride the gap between the landed aristocracy who have too much and the feudal serf who has too little; because only with such a middleclass, can we guarantee the stability and permanence of our democratic way of life.

With Fervor Burning

And it is to the credit of our economists that, in spite of foreign advice, they nagged, cajoled and practically forced into being the start of our Industrial Revolution.

During the last decade, a new dynamic class of entrepreneurs, titans of industry, finance and marketing, emerged upon the local scene, setting up local industries of fantastic diversity. Name it and it is being manufactured, processed or packaged by Filipino hands — from pins to ships and sealing wax, from soap to nuts and bolts.

Yet at the end of the 1960's, shortly before Macapagal took over, the momentum of industrialization slowed down to a walk, dropping from 8% annual increase in gross national product to a bare 2% annual increase. Why? Because of Import Controls, because of graft and corruption? That is the politician's answer.

The economist knows better. He knows that the initial spurt of industrialization began with the establishment of light industries manufacturing consumer goods from imported materials. He knows that the next step inevitably involves the setting up of intermediate and basic industries manufacturing raw materials for the consumption goods industries. He knows that such intermediate and basic industries needed much more capital than hitherto needed to achieve the same increase in gross national product; and that such capital was not forthcoming until the Controls ended.

He knows, most important of all, that such basic industries need to produce for a much larger market to be profitable; otherwise it must be protected artificially by high tariff walls.

With' modern technology, the optimum scale of operation in most basic industries, is already more than a market of 30 million can absorb. In such small countries as the Philippines, optimum size can only be achieved if firms enjoy a virtually monopolistic position.

In such a market, any attempt to promote competition results in overcrowding of industries, misallocation and waste of productive resources, and high cost highly cartelized domestic production.

It is not enough to industrialize, it is not enough that industrialization puts more people to work at higher wages; it is important as well to bring lower prices to the consumer. To promote faster industrialization and maximize its benefits to the man of the population, it is imperative that mass production techniques be employed under conditions of free competition.

And the only way for the Philippines to achieve this is to enlarge its consumer market beyond its borders, by sharing a common market with other nations.

AN ERA OF GIANTS

History has many examples of how great cities grow. When Greece and the Middle East were at the height of their glory, it was Troy that dominated the commerce of the world. Commerce shifted to the Mediterranean Sea, and political power shifted to Rome, later to Venice. Commerce then expanded to the Atlantic; and Cadiz, Lisbon, and London were the capitals of the world. New York and Boston grew, and as America marched to the West, Chicago and San Francisco came into their own. Trade routes to Asia fed the growing cities of Tokyo, Shanghai, Hongkong, and Bombay.

Those who are conscious of the tides of history and posterity, have reason to hope that the Philippines and its major cities — Manila and Cebu — are marked for future greatness. For, facing eastward to America and northward to Japan and China, they stand at the gateway to one of the world's richest unexploited areas.

With Fervor Burning

To the south and west lie rich markets and abundant resources awaiting the stroke of willing hands.

There is Malaysia, the richest country in per capita income in Asia aside from Japan, populated by ten million potential customers, prodigious with resources like tin, rubber and tungsten. There is Indonesia, a populous country of 103 million people rich with oil, rubber, and bauxite. Compared with these two countries, the Philippines has a 30-million population and has developed resources of iron, nickel, copper, chrome, manganese, and hemp.

Together, these three countries have a population base of 140 million people for a larger consumer market. Together, they have a common pool of complimentary raw material resources, all that is necessary for all-out industrial development. Together, they can develop into an economic and political force that may counter-balance the three colossi of the north, China, Japan and India. They can do this only by a kind of unity that can be achieved by a Pan-Malayan common market.

Actually, the idea of a common market is not new. Before 1781, the 13 American states under the Articles of Confederation, were separate economic units permitted to levy import duties against each other. After the American Revolution, the Constitution of the United States tore down these tariff barriers and forbade trade restrictions within the union without the consent of Congress.

Had the framers of the Constitution not exercised a vision and statesmanship to put an end to the loose economic bonds of the confederation in one stroke and without any transition period, the United States might have been another Balkanized Europe or another Latin America. Today the United States has a common market of more than 180 million people.

The lessons of history have not been lost to the rest of the world. The economic achievements of the 50 states of the union, the progress attained by the union of 15 Soviet Socialist Republics, the advances made by Japan's 90 million people, the rapid industrialization made by the unification of the 600 million people under the Red Chinese — all of these must have had something to do with the efforts of a forceful group of intellectual Europeans to constitute themselves into larger economic units.

In recent years we have seen the gradual establishment of three giant economic blocs in Europe alone.There is the voluntary association of six states including France and West Germany under the European Economic Community (EEC) with a population of 168 million people.

At the same time, seven countries along the periphery of Europe, including Great Britain and the Scandinavian countries, have constituted themselves into the European Free Trade Ares (EFTA) consisting of 90 million people.

Not to be outdone, six eastern European countries and Russia with a total population of 300 million people also combined their economies under the Soviet-sponsored Council of Mutual Economic Assistance (Comecon).

In Latin America, the Treaty of Monteviedo establishes a common market of seven nations — Brazil, Chile, Peru, Uruguay, Argentina, Mexico and Paraguay, with a potential market of 120 million consumers.

We, in this corner of the globe are being made to realize that as small nations, we live in an era of political and economic giants, that in order to survive and find a position of international strength and stature, we ourselves must seek unity with others in our own part of the world. We are being made to realize that if the goal of humanity is the brotherhood of man under a world government, then regional cooperation and unity must provide a natural and most logical transition to such a worthwhile goal.

THE COMMON MARKET IDEA

Mightier than the march of armies is an idea whosa hour has come.

Such an idea is on the march — the idea of a common market, a commonly shared market by many nations to promote economies of large-scale production particularly where national markets do not justify the establishment of optimum industrial units, taking advantage of joint industries among a group of nations particularly to produce heavy engineering and capital goods.

How shall such a common market be shared? A United Nations report details many forms of common market arrangements.

At one extreme is the economic union, in which goods, services, capital, and labor move freely without restrictions under one common economic policy; this eventually leads to common currency and political integration. An economic union is what the United States is today, and what the European Economic Community hopes eventually to be.

Some oppositors to the idea of the common market assume that the Common Market must necessarily be an economic and political union of states. It is not necessarily so, for a commonly shared market between states may take many forms, involving preference of one kind or another, entailing varying degrees of economic integrating and varying degrees of surrender of national sovereignty.

The European Economic Community, commonly known as the European Common Market, is not yet an economic union; it is, strictly speaking, at the present state, a customs union.

With Fervor Burning

The rival EFTA, or Outer Seven, led by Great Britain, as well as the Latin American Common Market under the Treaty of Montevideo, are horses of a different color; they are an example of what is known as a free trade area.

Both a customs union and a free trade area involve the establishment of a common market in "substantially all the trade" of the member countries, entailing the elimination of tariff and other restrictions of trade between the member countries.

The difference lies in this: In a customs union, the member countries adopt a common external tariff applicable to third countries; in a free trade area, the member countries may apply their own separate tariffs to non-member countries.

A fourth method of economic cooperation is the sectoral or partial integration, as exemplified by the European Coal and Steel Community, which provides for a common market only in one sector, i.e, coal and steel, instead of in "substantially all the trade" as in the case of the customs union.

A fifth method is the preferential application of quantitative restrictions, as exemplified by the OEEC (Organization for European Economic Cooperation), in which case, quantitative restrictions or quotas are progressively removed on intra-OEEC trade.

This again differs from a customs union, in that it involves the abolition of only quantitative restrictions on trade but not of customs duties, whereas a customs union would involve the abolition of both tariff duties and other trade restrictions.

A sixth method is the preferential application of tariff duties on trade among the member countries, such as exemplified by the British Commonwealth of Nations which extend mutual tariff preferences.

This, however, does not involve any progressive abolition of tariffs, but only allows a margin of preference in favor of goods of Commonwealth origin as against goods of other origin.

A seventh method, which is debatable, is the long-term trade contract which may theoretically promote some degree of economic coordination between countries.

Trade between Red China, Russia, and their satellites are largely conducted under five-year trade agreements in accordance with economic development programs of mutual benefit.

A common market a commonly shared market, may be achieved in many different ways depending on the proposed membership, their political attitudes and aspirations, and their comparative stages of development, with many possibilities open for a modest beginning through transitional stages to as close a cooperation as dared or desired.

The problem of seeking a common market partner for the Philippines in particular involves many special considerations:

To begin with, we must decide once and for all to shift from our traditional pattern of trade as a raw material supplier, and seek new markets to which we may sell the surplus products of our modem industries, and from which we may buy basic materials we lack.

From this we infer that it will do us no good to seek a common market with a nation more industrialized than we are. Our experience with the United States with whom we had an economic union for 50 colonial years, and a preferential application of quantitative restrictions under the Bell Trade Act and Laurel-Langley Agreement, proves, if it proves anything at all, that free trade between an industrial colossus and an under-developed country, is a one-way street with the poor at an extreme disadvantage.

Industrial development is impossible under the weight of unfair competition from the industrialized country. There is no dividend in it In succumbing to its temporary and short-run benefits, the underdeveloped country invites insult to compound the injury, such as parity and extra-territorial rights for the dominant partner.

By this token, we must reject any notion of preferential trade with Japan or the European Economic Community at our present stage of development.

If we must share a common market, it must be with a nation at a stage of development at least equal to ours... better still with a nation less developed than we are . . . preferably adjacent to our national borders, and populated with the same racial stock.

I can think of no better partners than Malaysia, Thailand, and Indonesia under the aegis of ASA and Maphilmdo.

PAN-MALAYAN COMMON MARKET

The greatest advantage of the Common Market is that it gives its members a solid foundation upon which to build a prosperous industrial economy based on (1) a strong domestic market, and (2) an adequate source of raw materials.

The United States has such an economy. So does Soviet Russia. And that's the reason why they are the greatest nations on earth today.

The entire economic structure of the United States is geared to produce for an internal market of 180 million consumers; only four per cent of its total production find their way into export markets. Russia itself has such a "home base" — a potential consumer market of 200 million people. Both Russia and the United States have adequate raw materials within their own national boundaries and spheres of influence to support their mighty industrial economies.

The desire for a large internal market and an adequate source of raw materials is the ulterior motive behind the dreams of conquerors — from Napoleon to Hitler, from the colonial empires of the last century to the American Manifest Destiny to the new communist imperialism.

But such a desire can also be achieved by voluntary co-operation and association. Witness now the British Commonwealth of Nations and the various European Common Markets. Consider now a pan-Malayan Common Market comprising the Philippines, Malaysia and Indonesia.

The Philippines, Malaysia and Indonesia together have a broad population base of some 143 million people and a common pool of complimentary raw material resources of oil and iron ore — the two sine qua non of industrial development. They have adequate resources of tin, bauxite, tungsten, copper, nickel, manganese and chorine; and such agricultural products as sugar, copra, rubber and hemp.

The three Malayan countries are all on the same level of development, all on the verge of industrialization. Free interplay of economic forces within their areas cannot but promote healthy industrial growth under the full stimulus of comparative advantage. Each country will specialize in the kind of products which it can manufacture efficiently with its skills and resources with an adequate base for mass production and mass marketing, and without the unfair competition of more technologically advanced countries.

The three Malayan countries are maritime nations whose seafaring peoples depend a great deal on the resources and trade lanes of the sea. But where are our fishing fleets? Where are our cargo ships and ocean liners? Even now, our export trade is dominated by a foreign cartel which fixes our freight rates at a higher level than comparative routes in Europe. These so-called "conference lines" constitute a monopolistic octopus that has on many occasions strangled our economic lifelines at their pleasure.

With Fervor Burning

A growing trade between the Pan-Malayan countries should stimulate the development of maritime fleets so necessary to the survival of the three. Our purchase of ocean-going vessels from Japan Reparations may be used, not to compete in established sea lanes but to explore the new trade routes of Pan-Malaya. Our ship-building industry can be geared to the inter-island needs of a much greater area. And perhaps, under the stimulus of a greater potential market, we can economically build fleets to exploit our tremendous fishing grounds, long poached upon by Japan.

Above all it is felt that with the formation of the Pan-Malayan Common Market, the Philippines has an opportunity to assert its leadership in this part of the world. Of the three Malayan countries, the Philippines has the highest literacy rate, the most active entrepreneurial class, the most developed fields of finance, marketing and industry. Not only that, we also have a surplus of engineers, teachers, doctors and other professionals, much needed in the other Malayan countries.

We have much to contribute to the Pan-Malayan countries, and we have much to benefit from them. The Pan-Malayan Common Market can well be, for the Philippines, a prelude to greatness.

AMERICANS DON'T ARGUE

We Filipinos are by nature argumentative. One may always see groups of people engaged in impassioned verbal jousts in the legislature on political platforms, in the schools and in club meetings. Open forums, symposiums and *balagtasans* are very much in the vogue. At the barrio level, we often witness heated arguments at the street comer, *sari-sari* store, public

With Fervor Burning

market, barbershop and even in the home where husband and wife often carry on a debate loud enough for all the neighbors to hear.

A Filipino who has studied abroad, invariably finds that his argumentative nature thrives best in the airy academic freedom of an American college .campus, where every idea meets the challenge of other ideas in free, open and unlimited debate. The best years of my life were spent in such a campus near Boston where, before a tableful of beer steins, we students and our professors argued till the wee hours of the morning about anything under the sun, our minds like free birds on the wing seeking Truth through unthinkable byways. With such a stimulating experience, I've always assumed that Americans are, as a general rule, as argumentative as Filipinos. I was wrong.

Shortly after I came back to the Philippines, in a party given by a group of young intellectuals, I met the local head of an American philanthropic foundation, who is presumably an educated man. Let's call him Mr. Smith. The party seemed like a throwback to the wonderful Boston days and as an opening gambit, we offered Mr. Smith some observations on Philippine-American relations. Then it happened.

"You Flips!" Mr. Smith cried. "We should have left you to the Japs! Listen, we pull outa here and you monkeys will be back climbing trees."

For quite a time after that and many similar experiences,

I started to conclude that local Americans do not argue with Filipinos because it is beneath their white man's dignity to do so. Again I was wrong.

A family friend. Professor Robert D. Glasgow, explained that Americans do not argue because they just do not know how. Mr. Smith did not mean to insult the Filipinos; he just gave vent to a personal frustration because of his total inability to conduct an intellectual discourse.

As the professor explained it, the average American, once he is out of the college campus, gets swallowed up by the mass culture of a highly organized society. He loses the art of making conversation — because his leisure hours are spent in mute hypnotic stupor before that "idiot box" he calls television. He does not read books, because comics are easier to read and besides, he can always look forward to seeing the movie version. He does not write letters because he can always pick up the telephone. Even the ritual of courtship by which we Filipinos learn to speak and write beautiful poetry, is denied the poor American; all he has to say to the lady is a completely prosaic "Hey, babe, let's have a good time, huh?"

On such world-shaking issues as peace end war, communism or the dilemma of the Asian in the modem world, the average American gets his opinions pre-formed and prepared in easily digestible capsules by TV commentators, gossip columnists, standard movie plots or the Time Magazine, much in the same way he gets his pre-cooked food and pre-fabricated houses. In the movies, for instance, William Holden needs no intelligent arguments to fight for God and Country. All he needs is a little sexual stimulation from a native girl, moonlight and roses, to solve singlehanded the problems of Asia in the American way.

The average American, according to Glasgow, is absolutely inarticulate; he cannot even communicate properly with his next-door neighbor — a fact that explains why Americans may live next door to each other for years without ever becoming acquainted.

Americans communicate with each other through a highly organized mass media of movies, magazines, newspapers, radio and the idiot box, whose regurgitations are necessarily formulated to the level of the lowest common denominator — about the intellectual level of a 12-year old child, which explains

With Fervor Burning

the kind of Cowboy-and-Indian mentality that divides the world into two hostile camps: the Subservients and the Subversives, with nothing in-between but no-man's-land.

As a result, continued Professor Glasgow, the American people distrust intelligence. Nothing is more fatal to an American politician seeking public office than to be accused of being an intellectual, an egghead, a long-hair. On the other hand, no matter how ignorant we Filipinos may be, at least we appreciate our intelligentsia. No Filipino politician would dare face the electorate until he can claim to be a bar-topnotcher, a scholar, a college graduate, or a recipient of numerous awards and testimonials.

The Comic Strip, which is one of America's greatest contributions to culture, reveals this American distrust of brains. Li'l Abner is a moron. Superman, a muscle-bound athlete with super physical powers, is the hero pitted against Luthor, the "mad scientist" Captain Marvel, Felix the Cat and every red-blooded American boy who reads them, vent their wrath on that legendary heel and villain, the "mad scientist" Nowhere else in the world is the scientist looked upon as a mad and evil thing. No wonder UJS. Nobel prize winners are almost always born and trained in Europe and elsewhere.

Americans, according to Glasgow, do not argue because they are inarticulate and distrustful of intelligence. Of course, he is not always right I have met many Americans since then who are both articulate and intelligent — among them, Ernest Neal and Jim Ingersoll of AID, John Esterline of USIA, some Peace Corps Volunteers, Robert Trumbull of New York Times, and a delightful chap named Bob Ballantyne, head of the Philippine desk at the U.S. State Deportment, who came to my office saying:

"Everytime I come to the Philippines, I get into the usual round of parties and meetings where Filipinos tell me what they think I want to hear. And I go back to

With Fervor Burning

Washington not knowing any more than I did when I first arrived. Mr. Henares, you have a reputation for saying what you mean. Care to have an argument?" And there followed one of the most intellectually stimulating afternoons of my life.

The mind is a wonderful thing — from it issue thoughts, words and ideas, by which is crystallized and expressed the sum total of man's creative and noble experience. It must be stimulated, honed to perfection by intellectual discourse. For minds are like rough diamonds — only by constant rubbing together may the luster be brought out.

With whom to argue? I can talk to Filipino intellectuals about sex, elections, the economy and most anything else except the one most important question of the day — Philippine-American relations.

When confronted with such a controversial subject, Filipino intellectuals react in either of two ways: (1) they look furtively around and hastily excuse themselves as if expecting the appearance of Stalin's police; or (2) they stare at me with beady unblinking eyes till I get the uncomfortable feeling that I have said a little too much to a CIA agent.

Perhaps then, the rules of the game dictate that a Filipino must discuss Phil-American relations only with brother Americans. So I seek out an American. And most of them react like a man we shall call Mr. Brown. He stares at me with the same beady unblinking eyes and says absolutely nothing — till I get the distinct impression that he is there not to argue withme, but to make a judgment on me; and that he will judge me not according to the logic of my arguments, but according to the motivations that impelled me to start the argument.

True enough, days later, I hear that Mr. Brown has been making the rounds of the cocktail party circuit revealing to all and sundry his solemn verdict on me.

If he disagreed with me (which is seldom), he

With Fervor Burning

would say "Whatsa matter with Henares? He is way out in left field!" If he agreed with me (which is often),he would say, "Hey, that Henares is okay, he should be a senator!"

One night I dreamt I was back in Boston, arguing again with my American schoolmates, my mind once more like a free bird on the wing, seeking Truth through unthinkable byways — then suddenly a steel trap snapped shut on my winging thoughts, my poor tortured mind now beating its broken wings against the inside of my skull, setting into motion waves of migraine pain against an overlapping montage of frightening images — those of Mr. Smith shouting his abominations and the Cocktail Circuit Judge Brown pronouncing his verdict like God Almighty — and I woke up with a cold sweat and a severe headache.

Sadly said I, as on the deathbed of an old and faithful friend: "Be still, my mind. Think no more. Yours is not to reason why. Yours is but to lie or die. May a thousand argumentative angels bear (or bore) you to your rest."

And to be sure my aching mind is laid to rest in peace, at least for the night — I flipped on the switch on the idiot box, tuned in on the late late show, and stared with beady unblinking eyes in mute hypnotic stupor, at the all-too-pat, all-too-simple, black-and-white answers of a William Holden movie to the unanswerable dilemma of an Asian trapped in the world of Pax Americana.

THE DILEMMA OF THE LAST FILIPINO

Rizal was the first Filipino, according to Leon Ma. Guerrero.

With Fervor Burning

Before Rizal, we were a conglomeration of many tribes which the Spaniards divided and ruled and called Indios. Bisayans fought the Tagalogs; Tagalogs, the Bikolanos; Pampangos, the Ilokanos; one tribe against another under Spanish command, for Spanish profit. We were made part of the Universal Church and the Spanish Empire.

It was Rizal who taught his countrymen that they could be something else, Filipinos who were members of a Filipino Nation, a narrower concept, more exclusive than the Universal Church or the Spanish Empire to which they were forced to owe allegiance — a Filipino nation embracing all tribes and serving the intents of its members above those of other nations.

Almost 70 yean have passed since the First Filipino met his martyrdom and set into motion the chain of events that led to what we now proudly proclaim to the world as the free and sovereign Republic of the Philippines.

Are we really a Nation, as envisioned by the First Filipino?

A few months ago, I received a poignant letter from a man who called himself the Last Filipino, who wrote:

We are fast losing our sense of nationhood. We are reverting back to ancient tribal loyalties — the Ilocano bloc set apart from the Bicol bloc, the Cebuano bloc, the Minsupala group. Even that is illusory.

For in truth and in fact, we have lost the sense of being part of something outside of and greater than ourselves, and have become a population of isolated individuals whose existence is bounded by birth and death, and whose primary concern is the interest of our own personal self.

As a result, we have become a vicious, selfish and greedy people — clawing and tearing at each other lor the little there is to hove — incapable of self sacrifice and united action for the greater glory of what we call our nation.

Hilarion (Larry) M. Henares Jr.   **110**

With Fervor Burning

Ours is probably the only nation on earth where nationalism is a dirty word. Ask any Japanese which is the greatest nation in the world; right or wrong, he will answer:Japan. The Germans feel the same way about Germany; the French about France; the Indons about Indonesia. "I am an American* is the proudest boast of an American. But ask a Filipino which is the greatest nation on earth and he will answer without hesitation: the United States of America.

For if the Filipino has any sense of identification outside of himself, it is with the United States of America. His tastes are "Stateside" and if he had any choice he would not be caught dead with the fruit of his own labor. His whole existence revolves around the Beatles, blue seal cigarettes, the Untouchables, White Christmas and Coca-cola.

His sense of identification with America is so complete, so overwhelming, that he feels superior to the Japanese, not because he thinks the Philippines is better than Japan but because he knows America is better than Japan.

One night during a party, I asked my friends two questions.

The first question: If it ever came to pass that the Philippines were at war with America, would you fight the Americans? (The Americans fought two warn against the British).

The unanimous answer was NO — because if such a war ever occurred, it must be the Communists who made it so.

The second question: If America were in a war the Philippines was not involved in, would you volunteer to fight America's enemies?

The unanimous answer was YES. For freedom and democracy, let us march to Armageddon!

"Traitors!" I cried. You have pledged your allegiance to other than your own country!"

"Who is the traitor and who is the patriot?" they countered. "What is treason after all, but the treachery of one against the interests of the many? If 99.9% of the Filipinos feel that their destiny lies with Mother America, and you feel otherwise, than you are the traitor!"

Hilarion (Larry) M. Henares Jr.   **111**

With Fervor Burning

I was unprepared for such an answer. For it involved me in a heartbreaking dilemma that haunts me every living minute.

Who is the traitor and who is the patriot? What am I?

Mr. Henares, I am a nationalist without a nation to fight for; I am a patriot without a country to love; I'm afraid I am, at least within the circle of my friends.

Yours truly,
The Last Filipino

You who call yourself The Last Filipino, let me tell you about the history of the Jewish race.

For two thousand years, they were the Wandering Jews, a people without a country, uprooted and tempest-tossed. They became British Jews, Polish Jews, Italian Jews, Arab Jews — no matter where they went, they were shunned and rejected even by those to whom they desperately offered their allegiance.

They became like us, isolated individuals bounded by birth and death, afloat on an ocean of nothingness, hanging on to every miserable piece of wreckage as if it were the tree of life.

As a result, the Jews were driven to desperate self-seeking — a vicious, greedy, selfish, miserly people, as the rest of the world pictured them — as Shakespeare's Shylock, demanding his pound of flesh; as Dicken's Fagin, teaching little boys how to cheat and steal.

All the tyrants in the world vented their fury against the Jews — but there were very few instances that the Jews were known to fight back. They allowed themselves to be herded into ghettos, driven into exile and massacred without fighting back, because they had nothing to fight for except their own isolated self, and they clung desperately to every minute of their miserable lives up to the very instant of oblivion.

When the British sought to exclude 600,000 Jews from Palestine after the last war, they had no reason to think the task would be difficult. For didn't Hitler easily take care of six million Jews in wartime Europe? What chance has 600,000 Jews against the whole British Empire and the surrounding sea of 60 million hostile Arabs?

But the British forgot one thing. The wandering Jews of Europe were isolated individuals without a sense of nationhood. The Jews in Palestine were an ancient people coming home to an ancient land, reviving the shattered dreams of two thousand years. They were part of something outside of themselves, they were part of something eternal, a chosen people who started life with Genesis and will continue to live till Judgment Day. They were a nation whose existence extends from the beginning to the end of time. The Jews in Palestine triumphed over the British and the Arabs, and proceeded to build a nation out of the sands of the desert For the Palestinean Jew, the present is a time of selfless labor to link a glorious past to an equally glorious future.

Yet there must have been times during the last two thousand years, when the dream was almost lost when 99.9% of the Jews felt that their allegiance belonged to other than the spirit of Jewish nationality.

Aham Haad, a Jewish thinker who must have felt as if he were the "Last Jew" among the Shy locks and Fagins, once wrote:

"If I feel in my heart the spirit of Jewish nationality so that it stamps my inner life with its seal, then the spirit of Jewish nationality exists. And its existence does not come to an end, even if all my Jewish contemporaries have ceased to feel it in their hearts."

This then is the answer to the dilemma of the Last Filipino:

If only one atom of matter exists in a totality of

nothingness that extends to the vastness of the infinite — then the universe exists — even if it exists in only in one single solitary atom of matter.

If one single candle flame burns in a totality of darkness that embraces a universe of cold stars and dead planets — then the warmth of that one single candle flame, no matter how feeble, can be felt in the farthest reaches of all creation.

And I say to you who call yourself theLast Filipino -- that if the spirit of Filipino nationalism exists within you — even if it exists nowhere else in this benighted land — for as long as you live, the Filipino Nation will never die.

---oOo---